起きてから寝るまで英語表現700
オフィス編 完全改訂版

オフィスでの「行為」「心のつぶやき」を全部英語で言う
➡会話力がみるみるアップ！

監修：吉田研作
執筆／解説：武藤克彦・荒井貴和

Preface

●以前とは大きく変化してきた職場環境

　世の中が目まぐるしく変わるに伴い、20年前と比べて、私たちの日常生活は大きく変化してきた。例えば、昔は通信手段といえば、電話とファクスが主流だったが、今や携帯電話、メール、インターネットなどに取って代わられている。昔、原稿を送るのに、バイク便をよく使った記憶があるが、今は、メールの添付ファイルであっという間に送ることができるようになった。

　物理的には20年前からは考えられなかったぐらい変化してきたわけだが、それは、多くの社会人がかかわっている会社内部での仕事内容、また、人間関係にどのような影響を及ぼしたのだろうか。確実に変化してきたのではないかと思われるのは、例えば、書類がデジタル化されてきたこと、そして、電話やインターネットを使った会議が増えてきたことが挙げられるだろう。私も経験があるが、国際会議を世界数カ国の人と同時に電話で実施できるとは昔は考えてもいなかった。モニターがあれば、議題や資料も見られる。そして、同時に気になるのは、人と面と向かう、という場面が減ってきたのかな、ということだ。スクリーンや電話の向こうで人とリアルタイムで「会う」ことができるのは素晴らしいことだが、直接会って話すのとは決して同じではない。

●人間同士が共感できるさまざまな表現

　そういう意味では、この「起き寝る」で扱っている表現も昔とはずいぶん変わってきている。例えば、cellphone、Internet、download、attachment、mail server、in-house bulletin、PDFなどは、この新しい通信手段の発達から生まれた用語である。だが、「起き寝る」で扱う用語や表現は変わっても、その基本的な考え方は変わらない。

はじめに

1）自分の行動を英語で言ってみる（I text my colleague.）
2）自分の置かれた状況等を英語にする（This room is full of computers.）
3）その時の自分の気持ちを英語で言ってみる
　（I feel so tired after answering so many e-mails.）
4）その時に考えたり感じたりしたことを英語にする
　（I'm not sure if this job is really what I wanted to do.）

「起き寝る」の基本的な考え方は、上記のような表現をひとりごととしてつぶやくことにより、ことばを自ら表す手段として使うことである。人によっては、自分の経験は自分だけのものだと思っているかもしれないが、一人の人の経験は、必ずほかの人のものともどこかで共通しており、共感できるものである。だから、本書に集められたさまざまな表現は、さまざまな人に当てはまる。「あるある。そうなんだよね。同じだ。なんだ、僕だけじゃなかったのか」と思う状況や経験が多々あるだろう。これは、世の中がどれだけ変わったとしても、同じ人間同士である以上、変わらないことなのである。

　さて、「起き寝る」は元々は、フランソワ・グワンが19世紀に開発した方法論を発展させたものだが、英語で自分の行動、まわりの描写、自分の気持ちや感じることを表現することにより、自らの表現力、発信力を伸ばすことが目的である。皆さんが本書の表現を使いながら、自らの英語力、英語表現力の向上にお役立ていただければ幸いです。

2010年2月　上智大学外国語学部英語学科教授　吉田研作

Contents
目次

はじめに　　　　　　　　P.2
本書の構成・使い方　　　P.6
付属CDの使い方　　　　P.10

chapter 1　内勤　Working at the Office
単語編/体の動き・行為/つぶやき表現/Skit/Quick Check　　**P.11**

chapter 2　人間関係　Human Relationships
単語編/体の動き・行為/つぶやき表現/Skit/Quick Check
会社組織関連語　　**P.43**

chapter 3　営業　Salesperson
単語編/体の動き・行為/つぶやき表現/Skit/Quick Check　　**P.73**

chapter 4　出張　Business Trips
単語編/体の動き・行為/つぶやき表現/Skit/Quick Check　　**P.99**

chapter 5　企画・開発　Planning & Development
単語編/体の動き・行為/つぶやき表現/Skit/Quick Check　　**P.123**

chapter 6 休 憩 Taking a Break
単語編/体の動き・行為/つぶやき表現/Skit/Quick Check **P.155**

chapter 7 会 議 Meetings
単語編/体の動き・行為/つぶやき表現/Skit/Quick Check **P.179**

chapter 8 社内行事 Company Events
単語編/体の動き・行為/つぶやき表現/Skit/Quick Check **P.209**

chapter 9 人事・待遇 Personnel Matters
単語編/体の動き・行為/つぶやき表現/Skit/Quick Check **P.229**

chapter 10 アフター5 After-Work Hours
単語編/体の動き・行為/つぶやき表現/Skit/Quick Check **P.259**

---

column
1. ビジネスシーンに必要なマナー&表現 　**P.68**
2. 基本的なビジネスメールの書き方 　**P.118**
3. ビジネスシーンでの効果的なプレゼンの仕方 　**P.204**

本書の構成と使い方
How to Use This Book

本書全体の構成と使い方

■出社からアフター5まで、一般的な会社員の1日を10章のシーンに分けています。

■それぞれの章は、「単語編」「体の動き・行為」「つぶやき表現」「Skit(会話)」「Quick Check(クイズ)」に分かれています。

■1章から順番にチェックしていくのもよし、または、自分の興味・状況に近いところから見ていくのもよいでしょう。

■オフィス内外のさまざまな英語表現を収録した本書で「つぶやき練習」を繰り返せば、ビジネスシーンで役立つスピーキング力を高めることができます。

各章(chapter)の構成と使い方

[単語編]

■ここでは、各シーンに関連する「物」や「事」を表す単語をイラストとともに掲載しています。単語のほとんどが後に続く「体の動き・行為」「つぶやき表現」の例文や解説に出てくるものです。

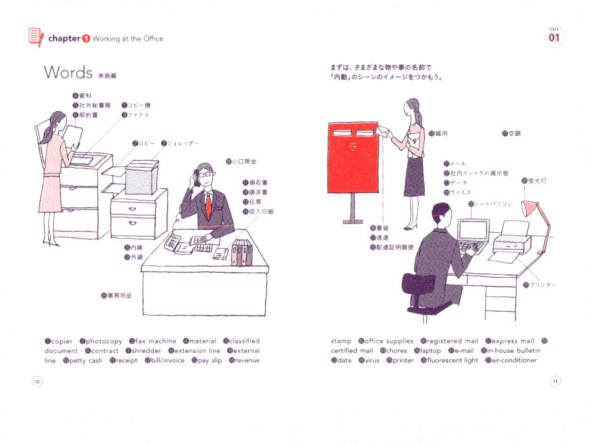

※まず、イラスト内の日本語を英語にできるかどうか試してみましょう。解答は下の欄に載っています。この単語編で、その章のイメージをつかみ、さまざまな英語表現に取り組む前のウォームアップをしましょう。

※付属CDにすべての単語が「日本語」→「英語」の順で録音されています。日本語をすぐに英語にする練習も試してみてください。

[体の動き・行為]

■ここでは、各シーンにおいて、毎日言葉にすることもなく、無意識に行っている行動・行為の数々を英語で紹介しています。これらの表現の多くは、一見簡単そうでいて、実はなかなか英語で言えないものです。オフィスでのこういった日常的な行動表現を、一つ一つ聞いたり、口に出したりしながら何度も練習し、自分のものにしていきましょう。

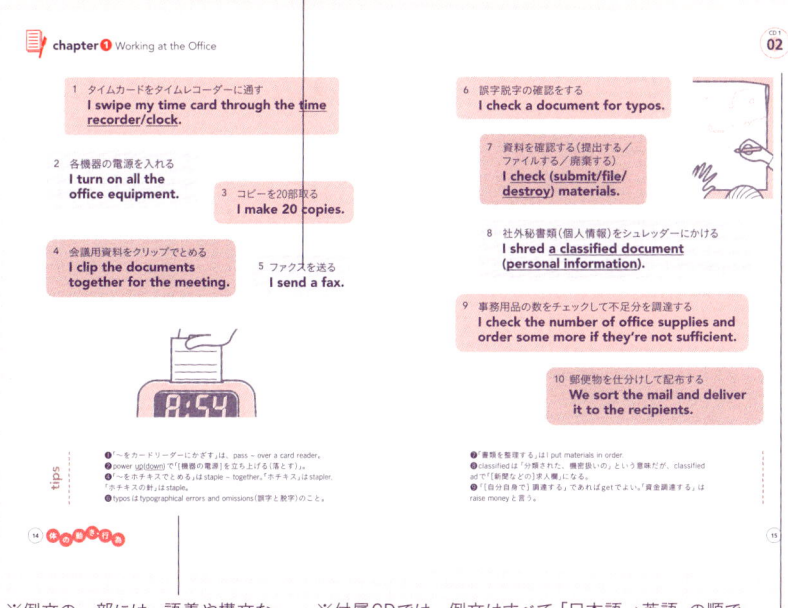

---

chapter ❶ Working at the Office

1. タイムカードをタイムレコーダーに通す
I swipe my time card through the time recorder/clock.

2. 各機器の電源を入れる
I turn on all the office equipment.

3. コピーを20部取る
I make 20 copies.

4. 会議用資料をクリップでとめる
I clip the documents together for the meeting.

5. ファクスを送る
I send a fax.

6. 誤字脱字の確認をする
I check a document for typos.

7. 資料を確認する（提出する／ファイルする／廃棄する）
I check (submit/file/destroy) materials.

8. 社外秘書類（個人情報）をシュレッダーにかける
I shred a classified document (personal information).

9. 事務用品の数をチェックして不足分を調達する
I check the number of office supplies and order some more if they're not sufficient.

10. 郵便物を仕分けして配布する
We sort the mail and deliver it to the recipients.

tips
❶「～をカードリーダーにかざす」は、pass ~ over a card reader.
❷ power up(down) で「(機器の)電源を立ち上げる(落とす)」。
❸「～をホチキスでとめる」は staple ~ together。「ホチキス」は stapler、「ホチキスの針」は staple。
❹ typos は typographical errors and omissions (誤字と脱字)のこと。

❼「書類を整理する」は I put materials in order。
❽ classified は「分類された、機密扱いの」という意味だが、classified ad で「(新聞などの)求人欄」になる。
❾「(自分自身で)調達する」であれば get でよい。「資金調達する」は raise money と言う。

※例文の一部には、語義や構文など表現への理解を手助けする解説（tips）が付いています。

※付属CDでは、例文はすべて「日本語→英語」の順で録音されています。本書を一通り学習したら、次は、日本語を聞いてすぐ英語にする練習をしてみてください。

さらにフレーズを記憶に定着させるには？

本CDに収録されている例文や会話を使って、シャドーイング練習してみましょう。シャドーイングとは、CDの音声を聞きながら、ほぼ同時に、耳でとらえたことを口で言う練習です。発音、リズム、イントネーションもそっくりまねると効果的です。最初はなかなかCDのスピードについていけないかもしれませんが、繰り返し練習するうちに、スムーズに口に出せるようになり、そのころには、単語・表現がすっかり自分のものとして身に付いているでしょう。

[つぶやき表現]

■「体の動き・行為」では、実際に外に表れる行動・行為の世界を言葉にしますが、ここでは、「内面」世界を扱います。行動する前、している最中、あるいはした後に、頭や心の中で考え、思っていることをどのように表現できるかを表しています。
こういったひとりごとの表現を使えば、「自分を中心とした内面世界を言語化」できます。そうすれば、通り一遍の会話表現では得られない、豊かで楽しい言語世界を味わえるでしょう。

※「つぶやき表現」の中には、自分の気持ちを伝える便利な表現としてそのまま他人との会話の中で使えるものもかなり入っています。ひとりごととして練習した後、実際に使ってみましょう。

※付属CDでは、例文はすべて「日本語→英語」の順で録音されています。本書を一通り学習したら、次は、日本語を聞いてすぐ英語にする練習をしてみてください。

---

chapter ❶ Working at the Office

1. ギリギリセーフ！ 間に合った！
   I made it! Just in time for work!

   make it = 間に合う／in time for ~ = ~に間に合う
   「~に遅れる」は be late for~。e.g. Hurry up! We're going to be late for the meeting. (急いで。会議に遅れちゃうよ。)。「時間通りに」は on time。e.g. The presentation started right on time. (プレゼンは時間通りに始まりました)

2. コーヒーメーカーを置くのはいいけど、片付けは男性もやってくださいね。
   I'm fine with the idea of installing a coffee maker, but could you guys please clean it up after using it?

   install = ~を設置する／clean - up を掃除する
   fine with は「~にとって問題ない、~は構わない」という意味。e.g. "So I'm going to lunch now." "Fine with me." 「じゃあ、先に昼食行きます」「構いませんよ。」

3. だれ、また空調強めたの？ クールビズだっちゅうの！
   Who cranked up the air-conditioner again? Don't you know what "Cool Biz" is?

   crank up - = ~を強める／Don't you know ~? = ~も知らないの(相手を軽く非難する表現)
   「~を強める」は turn up ~ の方が一般的だが、エアコンに「強弱」と温度の「上下」が絡らっているので、crank up ~ を用いた方がよい。反対は crank down ~ (~を弱める)。

4. いくらエコとは言え、廊下の蛍光灯取りすぎ。
   I know it's eco-friendly, but don't you think they've removed too many fluorescent lights in the hallway?

   eco-friendly = 環境に配慮した、エコな／fluorescent light = 蛍光灯／hallway = 廊下
   eco は ecology (生態系) のことだが、カタカナ語の「エコ」は eco-friendly (環境に優しい) を指す。e.g. eco-friendly packaging (transportation) (環境に配慮した包装＜交通手段＞)

5. 引き出しが古い資料でパンパン。そろそろ整理しなきゃ。
   My drawers are filled to capacity with old papers. Guess it's time to organize them.

   drawer = 引き出し／capacity = 容量／Guess ~ = ~と思う(= I guess ~)／organize = 整理する
   to capacity で「容量一杯まで、満員で」の意味。e.g. The hotel was booked to capacity because it was close to the convention venue. (会議場に近かったので、そのホテルは予約で一杯でした)

6. 書類が溜まってるから今日は腰をすえて一日社内で事務仕事だ。
   With all the documents that have piled up, I have to buckle down to office work all day today.

   With ~ = ~なので／pile up = 山積みになる／buckle down to ~ = ~に真剣に取り組む
   pile は名詞で「[書類などの] 山」の意味になる。e.g. My desk is always swamped with piles of documents. (いつも自分の机は書類の山で埋まってます)

※見出しの和文と英文は、必ずしも直訳の関係ではありません。こんな気持ちを英語らしく言おうとするとどういう表現になるのか、という例として挙げられています。

※それぞれの例文には、表現への理解を手助けするための解説が付いています。語義や構文を理解し、さらに発展的な語彙や表現を身に付けることができます。

[Skit]

■各章に出てきた表現を使った会話形式のストーリーです。実際の会話の流れの中で、学習した表現がどのように使えるのかを具体的に把握できます。表現を使いこなすための実践編として、登場人物になったつもりで繰り返し言ってみましょう。

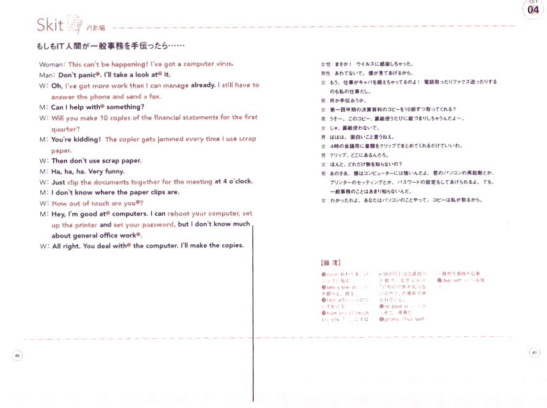

※「体の動き・行為」「つぶやき表現」に出てきた英語表現は赤紫色になっています。

[Quick Check]

各章に出てきたけれどもSkitには使われなかったフレーズを主に使っているクイズです。日本語の意味になるように、英文を完成させてください。わからなかったフレーズは、該当ページに戻って復習しましょう。

[本書の表記について]

本書は、特に記述のない限り、アメリカ英語の表記・音声を収録しています。そのほか、記号については下記を参照してください。

cf.	以下を参照
e.g.	以下は例文
___/___	スラッシュの前後の下線部は入れ替えても同じ意味
[ ]	[ ]内の語句を付け足してもよい
( )	( )内の語句に替えてもよい(意味は異なる)

付属CDの使い方　Directions for the CD

■本文CDマークでトラック番号を確認

本書にはCDが2枚付いています。音声を聞くときは、各項目の最初に掲載されているCDトラックの番号を呼び出してご利用ください。

■CDトラックマーク

CD1 **01** 各項目に付いているこのマークの数字が、付属CDのトラック番号に対応しています。

■収録内容

単語編
体の動き・行為
つぶやき表現
Skit

■収録分数

1枚目：約55分
2枚目：約50分

■収録言語

日本語　英語
→すべてのフレーズが日本語と英語で収録されています。フレーズを一通り理解した後には、日本語を聞いたらすぐに英語が口を突いて出てくるようになるまで繰り返し練習しましょう。

■トラック表

1枚目

章	ページ	トラック
chapter 1	012-041	**01-04**
chapter 2	044-071	**05-08**
chapter 3	074-097	**09-12**
chapter 4	100-121	**13-16**
chapter 5	124-153	**17-20**

2枚目

章	ページ	トラック
chapter 6	156-177	**01-04**
chapter 7	180-207	**05-08**
chapter 8	210-227	**09-12**
chapter 9	230-257	**13-16**
chapter 10	260-281	**17-20**

※CD取り扱い注意
●弊社制作の音声CDは、CDプレーヤーでの再生を保証する規格品です。
●パソコンでご使用になる場合、CD-ROMドライブとの相性により、ディスクを再生できない場合がございます。ご了承ください。
●パソコンでタイトル・トラック情報を開示させたい場合は、iTunesをご利用ください。iTunesでは、弊社がCDのタイトル・トラック情報を登録しているGracenote社のCDDB(データベース)からインターネットを介してトラック情報を取得することができます。
●CDとして正常に音声が再生できるディスクからパソコンやmp3プレーヤー等への取り込み時にトラブルが生じた際は、まず、そのアプリケーション（ソフト）、プレーヤーの製作元へご相談ください。

chapter 1

内 勤
Working at the Office

朝出社してタイムカードを押す、
電話を取る、書類を扱う、
パソコンを操作する——
さまざまな業種に共通する
普遍的なオフィスワークに携わる人々の
体の動きや行為、心のつぶやきです。

chapter 1 Working at the Office

Words 単語編

- ❶ コピー機
- ❷ コピー
- ❸ ファクス
- ❹ 資料
- ❺ 社外秘書類
- ❻ 契約書
- ❼ シュレッダー
- ❽ 内線
- ❾ 外線
- ❿ 小口現金
- ⓫ 領収書
- ⓬ 請求書
- ⓭ 伝票
- ⓮ 収入印紙
- ⓯ 事務用品

❶copier ❷photocopy ❸fax machine ❹material ❺classified document ❻contract ❼shredder ❽extension line ❾external line ❿petty cash ⓫receipt ⓬bill/invoice ⓭pay slip ⓮revenue

12

まずは、さまざまな物や事の名前で
「内勤」のシーンのイメージをつかもう。

⑲ 雑用
㉗ 空調
㉑ メール
㉒ 社内イントラの掲示板
㉓ データ
㉔ ウイルス
㉖ 蛍光灯
⑳ ノートパソコン
⑯ 書留
⑰ 速達
⑱ 配達証明郵便
㉕ プリンター

stamp ⑮office supplies ⑯registered mail ⑰express mail ⑱certified mail ⑲chores ⑳laptop ㉑e-mail ㉒in-house bulletin ㉓data ㉔virus ㉕printer ㉖fluorescent light ㉗air-conditioner

chapter ❶ Working at the Office

1 タイムカードをタイムレコーダーに通す
I swipe my time card through the <u>time recorder</u>/<u>clock</u>.

2 各機器の電源を入れる
I turn on all the office equipment.

3 コピーを20部取る
I make 20 copies.

4 会議用資料をクリップでとめる
I clip the documents together for the meeting.

5 ファクスを送る
I send a fax.

tips
❶「~をカードリーダーにかざす」は、pass ~ over a card reader。
❷power <u>up</u>(<u>down</u>)で「[機器の電源]を立ち上げる(落とす)」。
❹「~をホチキスでとめる」はstaple ~ together。「ホチキス」はstapler,「ホチキスの針」はstaple。
❻typosはtypographical errors and omissions(誤字と脱字)のこと。

6 誤字脱字の確認をする
I check a document for typos.

7 資料を確認する(提出する／ファイルする／廃棄する)
I <u>check (submit/file/destroy)</u> materials.

8 社外秘書類(個人情報)をシュレッダーにかける
I shred <u>a classified document (personal information)</u>.

9 事務用品の数をチェックして不足分を調達する
I check the number of office supplies and order some more if they're not sufficient.

10 郵便物を仕分けして配布する
We sort the mail and deliver it to the recipients.

- ❼「書類を整理する」はI put materials in order.
- ❽classifiedは「分類された、機密扱いの」という意味だが、classified adで「[新聞などの]求人欄」になる。
- ❾「[自分自身で]調達する」であればgetでよい。「資金調達する」はraise moneyと言う。

chapter ❶ Working at the Office

11 電話を取る
I answer the phone.

12 内線をかける
I call someone at his extension.

13 受けた電話の伝言を伝える
I pass on a message I took [for someone].

14 電話を保留にする
I put the call on hold.

15 仕事の流れを把握する
I make sure of the workflow.

tips

⓫「電話を取る」はpick up the phoneとも。「電話に出る」はget the phone。
⓬「外線」はexternal line。e.g. Please dial 0 first for an external number.（外線はゼロ発信してください）
⓭ leave a message with~ で「~に伝言を残す」。
⓯「合理化する」はstreamline。e.g. We'll streamline our operations.（業

16 業務の見直しをして、無駄な作業を省く
I review the workflow to eliminate unnecessary jobs.

17 稟議書を回す
We circulate a *ringi*, a document to get approval for a decision.

18 書類に上司のサイン(判子)をもらう
I have my boss <u>sign</u> (<u>stamp</u>) the documents.

19 契約書に割り印を押す
I affix a seal over two edges of the contract.

20 デスク回りをきれいに(清潔に)保つ
I keep my desk <u>organized</u>(<u>clean</u>).

務を合理化します)
⑱「判子を押す」は put the official seal on a document。
⑲ seal は「押印、捺印」「押印する」の意味。stamp より正式な場面で使われる。日本語で言う「シール」は sticker。
⑳「机(の上)を整理する」は I clear my <u>desk(desktop)</u>.。

chapter ① Working at the Office

21 小口現金の管理をする
I keep track of the petty cash.

22 伝票を切る
I issue a pay slip.

23 経費を申請する
I claim my expenses.

24 お客様を応接室にご案内する
I show a guest to the drawing room.

25 ロビーで接客する
I meet a guest in the lobby.

tips

㉑「帳簿をつける」は keep <u>books</u>/<u>accounts</u>。
㉓「経費の申請書を出す」は I submit an application for my expenses.。
㉕「訪問客を入り口で見送る」は I send the guest off at the entrance.。
㉗ budget proposal for the next fiscal year で「次年度の予算案」。
㉘ tally(集計する)を使い I tally sales figures. と言ってもよい。

体の動き・行為

26 事業計画を作る
I make a business plan.

27 予算案を作成する
I make a budget plan.

28 売上を集計する
I work out/calculate total sales.

29 決算報告をする
I announce the financial results.

30 社長決裁をとる
I ask for a final decision from the president.

㉙「決算報告書」は final statements、「決算期」は accounting term と言う。
㉚ I submit something for the president's approval. で「社長決裁を仰ぐ」。

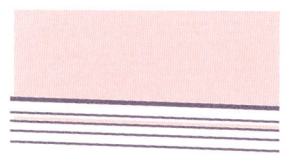

chapter ① Working at the Office

31 パソコンを立ち上げる
I start up my computer.

32 ウイルスチェックをする
I scan for viruses.

33 メールをチェックする(送る)
I <u>check(send)</u> my mail.

34 社内[イントラ]の掲示板をチェックする
I browse the in-house bulletins.

35 パスワードを設定する
I set the password.

tips

㉛「パソコンを再起動する」はI reboot my computer.。
㉜ keep the virus-checking software up to date で「ウイルスチェックソフトを最新のものにしておく」。
㉝「〜のメールに返信する」はanswer someone's mail、「メールを転送する」はforward the e-mail と言う。

体の動き・行為

36 プリンターを設定する
I set up a printer.

37 イントラから書類をダウンロードする
I download documents from the intranet website.

38 資料をPDFに変換する
I convert the document to a PDF.

39 データを整理する
I sort the data.

40 パソコンの不具合を担当部署に連絡する
I contact the department in charge about a problem on my computer.

㉞ browse は「〜をざっと見る、ネットを閲覧する」の意味。
㊱ set a printer to a high resolution で「プリンターを高解像度に設定する」。
㊴ sort は「振り分ける」「分類する」という意味合い。「データベースからデータを引っ張ってくる」は extract the data from a database。

chapter ❶ Working at the Office

1. ギリギリセーフ！ 間に合った！
I made it! Just in time for work!

2. コーヒーメーカーを置くのはいいけど、片付けは男性もやってくださいね。
I'm fine with the idea of installing a coffee maker, but could you guys please clean it up after using it?

3. だれ、また空調強めたの？ クールビズだっちゅうの！
Who cranked up the air-conditioner again? Don't you know what "Cool Biz" is?

4. いくらエコとは言え、廊下の蛍光灯取りすぎー。
I know it's eco-friendly, but don't you think they've removed too many fluorescent lights in the hallway?

5. 引き出しが古い資料でパンパン。そろそろ整理しなきゃ。
My drawers are filled to capacity with old papers. Guess it's time to organize them.

6. 書類が溜まっているから今日は腰をすえて一日社内で事務仕事だ。
With all the documents that have piled up, I have to buckle down to office work all day today.

make it = 間に合う／in time for ~ = ~に間に合う

「~に遅れる」は be late for~。e.g Hurry up! We're going to be late for the meeting.（急いで。会議に遅れちゃうよ）。「時間通りに」は on time。 e.g. The presentation started right on time.（プレゼンは時間通りに始まりました）

---

install ~ = ~を設置する／clean ~ up = ~を掃除する

fine with ~ は「~にとって問題ない、~は構わない」という意味。e.g. "So I'm going for lunch now." "Fine with me."「じゃあ、先に昼食行きます」「構いませんよ」

---

crank up ~ = ~を強める／Don't you know ~? = ~も知らないの（相手を軽く非難する表現）

「~を強める」は turn up ~ の方が一般的だが、エアコンは「強弱」と温度の「上下」が紛らわしいので、crank up ~ を用いた方がよい。反対は crank down ~（~を弱める）

---

eco-friendly = 環境に配慮した、エコな／fluorescent light = 蛍光灯／hallway = 廊下

eco は ecology（生態系）のことだが、カタカナ語の「エコ」は eco-friendly（環境に優しい）を指す。e.g. eco-friendly packaging (transportation)（環境に配慮した包装＜交通手段＞）

---

drawer = 引き出し／capacity = 容量／Guess ~(= I guess ~) = ~と思う／organize = 整理する

to capacity で「容量一杯まで、満員で」の意味。e.g. The hotel was booked to capacity because it was close to the convention venue.（会議場に近かったので、そのホテルは予約で一杯でした）

With ~ = ~なので／pile up = 山積みになる／buckle down to ~ = ~に真剣に取り組む

pile は名詞で「[書類などの] 山」の意味になる。e.g. My desk is always swamped with piles of documents.（いつも自分の机は書類の山で埋もれてます）

chapter 1 Working at the Office

7 第一四半期の決算資料コピー10部よろしく。
Will you make 10 copies of the financial statements for the first quarter?

8 いつも人に頼んでばかり。たまには自分でコピーくらいしてほしい。
He's always asking me to do things for him. Can't he make a photocopy once in a while?

9 裏紙使うといっつもコピーつまっちゃうんだよね〜。
The copier gets jammed every time I use scrap paper.

10 なんだかコピー機の調子が悪いみたい。急いで修理に来てもらわなきゃ。
Looks like something's wrong with the copier. I should ask maintenance to come right away.

11 ファクスが送信エラーで送れてなかった。
My fax message couldn't be sent because of a transmission error.

12 最近小さい文字が見えにくいんだけど……ひょっとして老眼?!
I'm having trouble reading small print these days …Are my eyes getting that old?

Will you ~? = ~して下さい／make copies of ~ = ~のコピーをとる／financial statements = 決算報告書／first quarter = 第1四半期

「鮮明な（不鮮明な）コピー」は <u>clean</u>(smudgy) copy と言う。また、copy onto A4 paper (A4にコピーする)、set the copier for 80 percent reduction (コピー機を80％縮小にセットする) もよく使う表現。

---

make a photocopy = コピーを取る／once in a while = たまには

once in ~ は「~において一度」。once in a while で「しばらくの間で1回→時々は」の意味になる。once in a lifetime (一生に1回)、once in a blue moon (めったに~ない) という表現もある。e.g. This may be a once-in-a-lifetime chance. (千載一遇のチャンスかも)

---

copier = コピー機／get jammed = [コピー用紙などが]詰まる／every time ~ = ~するたびに／scrap paper = 捨て紙、裏紙

「紙づまり」は paper jam と言う。e.g. It took me 30 minutes to print 20 pages because of paper jam. (紙づまりのせいで20ページ印刷するのに30分かかった)

Looks like ~ = ~のようだ／maintenance = 修理担当の方

something is wrong with ~ は「~の調子が悪い」の意味。「[事務機器が]壊れている」は out of order。e.g. You can't use the fax machine because it's out of order. (そのファクスは使えないよ。故障中だから)

---

transmission error = 送信エラー（delivery errorとも言う）

「ファクスを受信する」は receive a fax message。また「~をファクスする」は fax ~、「~にファクスを送る」は send ~ a fax でよい。なお「ファクス［から出てきた］紙を破り取る」は pull the piece of paper off the fax と言う。

---

have trouble ~ing = ~に苦労する／small print = 細かい文字

「老眼の、遠視の」は far-sighted、「老眼鏡」は far-sighted glasses と言う。e.g. I think I'm becoming far-sighted because of my age. (年のせいで老眼になってきたみたいだ)

chapter ① Working at the Office

13 収入印紙のストックが少ないから、郵便局で買って来よう。
I only have a few revenue stamps in stock, so I'll go get some at the post office.

14 この書類を書留で発送しておいてくれる?
Have this document sent by registered mail, will you?

15 この書類、社外秘(個人)情報を含むから、取り扱いに気をつけてね。
Make sure you look after this document because it contains <u>classified</u>(<u>personal</u>) information.

16 最近の新人は、電話の受け答えがなってないね。
Recruits these days can't even have a proper telephone conversation, can they?

17 新人はもっと積極的に電話を取らなきゃ。昔はワンコールで出るよう、しつけられたものだけど。
New recruits should be answering the phone first. We used to be taught to pick up the phone on the first ring.

18 最近クレーム続きだから電話を取るのもドキドキだよ。
Since we've been having a lot of customer complaints recently, just picking up the phone gives me butterflies in my stomach.

in stock = 在庫のある、残っている／post office = 郵便局

stock は「在庫」の意味。「在庫が切れている」は out of stock と言う。e.g. Staples are out of stock, so we should call the supplier.（ホチキスの針の在庫がないので、納入業者に電話しないと）

---

have ~ sent = ~を送ってもらう／registered mail = 書留郵便

「時間指定で郵送する」は mail ~ at a specified time、「速達（配達証明）で送る」は send ~ by express(certified) mail と言う。e.g. I'd like to send this by express mail.（これを速達で送りたいのですが）

---

make sure S+V = 必ずS+Vであることを確認する／look after ~ = ~に注意する／classified = 機密の、社外秘の

「~を注意深く取り扱う」は handle ~ with care でもよい。e.g. Confidential data should be handled with care.（機密のデータは注意深く取り扱われるべきです）

---

recruit = 新入社員／these days = 最近は／have a telephone conversation = 電話で会話をする

ここでの proper は business-like（実務的な、ビジネスの）のこと。e.g. You should know the difference between a business conversation and a private chat with friends.（仕事上の会話と友人との私的なおしゃべりの違いを知っておくべきだよ）

---

answer the phone = 電話に出る／pick up the phone = 電話を取る／on the first ring = ワンコールで

on the first ring は「電話のコール音1回で」の意味。cf. Hang up your cellphone after one ring so I can get your phone number.（1回鳴らしたら携帯切ってよ。それで電話番号わかるから）

---

customer complaint = 顧客からのクレーム／give ~ butterflies in one's stomach = ~をドキドキさせる

butterflies in one's stomach は「胃の中でチョウが飛んでいる感じ」から「[発表など重要な場面の直前で] そわそわする、落ち着かない」の意味。e.g. I've got butterflies in my stomach.（緊張してます）

chapter ❶ Working at the Office

19 突然の外国人からの電話にすごく焦った。
That sudden phone call from a non-Japanese surprised the hell out of me.

20 取扱商品についての問い合せ？　営業部に電話を回して対応してもらって。
An inquiry about our product? Transfer the call to the sales department and let them deal with it.

21 あそこの課の内線って何番だったっけ？
I wonder what the extension number of that section is.

22 あの会社、とにかくいつも電話がつながらない！
No matter when I call, I can never get through to that company.

23 今日は仕事がサクサク進むぞ。気持ちいいな。
My job is going without a hitch today. I feel so good.

24 月末はいろんなものの締切が重なるなあ。
A number of deadlines overlap at the end of every month.

non-Japanese = 日本人ではない人、外国人（foreignerよりは丁寧な言い方）／surprise the hell out of ~ = ~をものすごく驚かせる

the hell out of は「大変、めちゃくちゃに」という意味の強調表現。口語的なので、同僚など親しい仲間内で使う方がよい。e.g. The movie scared the hell out of me.（その映画はめちゃくちゃ怖かったよ）

---

inquiry = 問い合わせ、紹介／transfer ~ to ... = ~を…に転送する／sales department = 販売部／deal with ~ = ~に応対する

inquire about ~ で「~について問い合わせる」。e.g. I'm calling to inquire about your Internet services.（御社のインターネットサービスについてお尋ねしたくお電話しております）

I wonder ~ = ~なのだろうか？／extension number = 内線／section = 部署

「[社内の通話料がかからない] 内線電話」は house phone と言う。e.g. Please use the house phone in the meeting room to call me.（会議室にある内線電話を使って私に電話してください）

No matter when ~ = いつ~しても／get through to ~ = ~につながる

put ~ through to ... で「~の電話を…につなげる」の意味。会社の代表電話番号にかけた後などに「経理部につないでください」と頼むときは Will you put me through to the accounting department? と言う。

---

without a hitch = スムーズに

go ＋副詞［句］で「~という状態で進行する、物事が運ぶ」の意味。e.g. Everything is going well.（万事うまくいっている）。without a hitch は「[作業が] 滞りなく、スムーズに」の意味の副詞句。hitch は「障害、引っかかり」。

---

a number of ~ = 複数の~、多くの~／deadline = 締切／overlap = 重なる

meet(miss) the deadline で「締切に間に合わせる（を逃す）」。また「締切」は due（~が期限の）を使って、This report is due on Friday.（この報告書は金曜に締切だ）のように表現する。

chapter ❶ Working at the Office

25 今日は、雑用が立て込んでいて落ち着かないなぁ。
I can't catch a break with the endless parade of chores today.

26 ちゃっちゃと終わらせて、次の作業に入らなきゃ。
I better get it over with now, and go on to the next task.

27 彼女、仕事がキャパを超えてるよ。
She's got more work than she can manage.

28 上司に承認してもらわないと、次の行動に移れないんだけど。
I can't move on to the next action without my boss's permission.

29 「今日中によろしく」って言われても……
It's easy for him to say "Get this done by the end of the day," but...

30 隣の人の独り言がうるさくて、仕事に集中できないよ。
The guy next to me is talking to himself so loudly I can't concentrate on my work.

can't catch a break = 息をつく暇もない／endless parade of ~ = 終わりのない一連の~／chores = 雑用、雑務

catch one's breath（息をつく）、get one's second wind（一息入れて元気回復する）もよく使う表現。e.g. I got my second wind after taking a coffee break.（コーヒーブレイクで一息ついて元気が出た）

I better ~ = ~しないとまずいな

get it over with は、finish（終わらせる）より、嫌なことや面倒くさいことを「[さっさと] 片付ける、やっつける」の意味合いが強い表現。e.g. Let's get it over with and have a break.（さっさとやっつけて休憩しよう）

---

manage = 何とかやりくりする

直訳すると「彼女は自分でやりくりできる以上の仕事を抱えている」という意味になる。「やりくりする」は handle でもよい。e.g. Let me handle this one.（この件は私にやらせてください）。

---

move on to ~ = ~に進む／permission = 許可、承認

「承認を求める（得る）」は ask for(get) someone's approval と言う。e.g. You have to get your boss's approval to take a vacation.（休暇を取るには上司の承認を得なければなりません）

---

it's easy for him to ~=彼が~するのは簡単だ／get ~ done = ~を終わらせる／by the end of the day=今日の終わりまでに

「[人] を意のままに動かす、~をあごで使う」は have ~ at one's beck [and call] と言う。e.g. The boss always has his staff at his beck.（あの上司はいつも部下をあごで使っている）。

---

talk to oneself = 独り言を言う／loudly = 大声で／concentrate on ~ = ~に集中する

「~にイライラする」は be irritated。e.g. I'm really irritated because someone around me keeps tapping his foot.（周りにいるだれかがずっと貧乏ゆすりしてるから、こっちまでイライラするよ）

chapter ❶ Working at the Office

31 主任は、ほんとに仕事さぼるのがうまい。
The chief sneaks out of his duties really well.

32 変更が発生したら、その都度ご連絡ください。
Please inform us every time there's a change.

33 GWは、うちはカレンダー通りに営業するよ。
During the Golden Week holidays, we'll do business as usual according to the calendar.

34 今日は伝票締切日。残業しないで終わらせよう！
Today is the last day for accepting pay slips. I'm going to finish off my work without doing overtime.

35 こんな領収書じゃ、経費は認められません！
You can't claim expenses with that kind of receipt.

36 早く請求書回してくれないかな。
Why are they taking so long to pass their invoices on to me?

sneak out of ~ = ~からコソコソ逃げ出す、さぼる

「サボる」という意味では goof off もよく使われる。e.g. I happened to catch the manager goofing off in the cafeteria.（偶然、社食で部長がサボっているのを見つけちゃった）

---

inform ~ = ~に知らせる／every time ~ = ~のたびに

「~に常に最新情報を与える、逐次連絡する」は keep ~ informed/posted と言う。e.g. Please keep me posted on the progress.（進捗状況については逐次連絡してください）

---

during ~ = ~の間中／do business = 営業する／as usual = 通常通りに／according to ~ = ~に従って

「暦年（1月1日〜12月31日）」は calendar year、「会計年度」は fiscal year と言う。e.g. Your contract is renewable according to the fiscal year.（会計年度に従って、契約更新が可能です）

---

pay slip = 支払伝票／finish off ~ = ~を終わらせる／overtime = 残業

do/work overtime で「残業して働く、超過勤務する」の意味になる。「定時に退社する」は leave the office on time。また、「9時5時の定時の仕事」は 9-to-5 job と言う。

---

claim ~ = ~を要求する／expenses = 経費／receipt = 領収書

「経費をごまかす」は juggle/cheat on expenses と言う。e.g. They say Mr. Gread often cheats on his travel expenses.（グリードさんはよく出張費をごまかしているらしい）

---

why ~ = なぜ~なのか?(非難のニュアンス)／take long to ~ = ~するのに時間がかかる／pass ~ on to ... = …に~を回す、渡す／invoice = 請求書

「すべきことを先延ばしにする、ぐずぐずする」は procrastinate、またそうする人を procrastinator と言う。e.g. You shouldn't procrastinate about organizing your desk.（机の整理するのを先延ばしにしない方がいいよ）

chapter ❶ Working at the Office

37 請求額が間違ってるよ。訂正してもらわなきゃ。
There's an error on the invoice. I should have it corrected.

38 お金のやり取りはもっと慎重にしなきゃ！
You've got to be more careful when dealing with money.

39 今、決算時期だから、寝る間もないくらい忙しい。
We're right in the middle of an accounting period, and it's been so hectic that I can barely sleep.

40 やっぱり、最低限のパソコン操作（ワードやエクセル）ができないと話にならないよね。
You're basically considered useless if you don't have good computer skills (can't use Word and Excel).

41 エクセルで表作ってるんだけど、誰か関数得意な人いない？
Is anyone good at functions ? I'm working on an Excel spreadsheet now.

42 データ入力もたまだと気分転換になるけどね。
Inputting data on a computer is good for a change ... if it's only once in a while.

have ~ corrected = ～を訂正してもらう

ビジネスレターで「訂正した請求書をお送りください」は Please send us the correct invoice.、「訂正した請求書を同封させていただきました」は Enclosed is a corrected invoice. と書く。

've got to ~(= have to do) = ～しなきゃならない／deal with ~ = ～を取り扱う／when dealing ~ = when you are dealing ~

「お金のやりとり」は giving and taking money でもよい。e.g. You cannot be too careful when giving and taking money.（金銭の授受においてはいくら注意しても、しすぎることはない）

---

accounting period = 決算期／so ~ that… = とても～なので…／hectic = 慌ただしい／can barely ~ = かろうじて～できる

「決算期」は fiscal term とも言う。「[忙しくて] 毎日残業続きだ」なら [so hectic] that I have to work overtime every day になる。

---

basically = 基本的に／be considered ~ = ～とみなされる

useless は「役に立たない、使えない」の意味。逆に「即戦力になる」は work-ready。e.g. Generally, companies are seeking [for] work-ready graduates.（概して企業は即戦力となる大卒を求めています）

---

function = 関数／work on ~ = ～に取り組んでいる／spreadsheet = 表計算[ソフト]

「～が得意な」は be good at ~ が一般的。one's cup of tea（自分のお茶）を使った表現もあるがこれはほとんどの場合、否定文で使う。e.g. Functions are not my cup of tea.（関数は自分の苦手分野だ）。Word のような「ワープロソフト」は word-processing software と言う。

---

input = 入力する／change = 変化、気分転換

「気分転換に」は for a change [of pace] と言う。e.g. Why don't we take a short walk around the building for a change?（気分転換に社屋の周りを少し散歩しませんか）

chapter 1 Working at the Office

43 新システムの構築には手こずったなあ。
I had a hard time establishing the new system.

44 私用メールは禁止だよ！
No private e-mails, OK?

45 わからないことが出てきたら、ググっちゃえ！
I just google what I don't know.

46 パソコンが固まった！ こんなことしてる時間はないのに。
My computer froze again! I don't have time for this!

47 まさか、ウイルスに感染した？
This can't be happening! I've got a computer virus?

48 PCがクラッシュしてデータが消えちゃった！ バックアップ取っておけばよかった！
My computer crashed and the data's gone. I should've backed it up.

have a hard time ~ing = ~するのに苦労する／establish = 構築する

「~に手こずる」は have difficulty/trouble with ~ を使ってもよい。e.g. We had trouble with rearranging all the files.（全ファイルの再整理には手こずりました）。find it hard going to ~（~が遅々として進まないと感じる）も使える。e.g. I found it hard going to rearrange all the files.

---

private = 私用の

No ~ で「~は禁止」の意味。掲示では No ~ allowed（~は禁止されています）もよく使われる。e.g. No food or drink allowed here.（ここでの飲食は禁止されています）、No recording allowed.（録音は禁止されています）、No pets allowed.（ペットは禁止です）

---

google = [主にGoogleを使って]検索する（動詞として使われる）

google（ググる）は検索エンジンの商標 Google が動詞に転用された単語。「検索したい語を入力します」は I type in the word I want to search for.、「検索してもわかりませんでした」は I did a search but couldn't find anything. と言う。

---

freeze = [パソコンが]固まる、フリーズする（frozeはfreezeの過去形）

「起動時にフリーズする」は freeze during startup、「原因不明で強制終了する」は shut down for no reason、「サーバーが落ちてしまった」は The server has crashed. と言う。

---

can't be ~ing = ~しているわけがない

パソコンが「ウイルスに感染する」は get infected by a computer virus と言う。また「ウイルスを駆除する」は get rid of a computer virus。

---

should've ~ (= should have) = ~しておくべきだった／back ~ up = ~のバックアップを取る

「データが修復できない、リカバリー不可能」は The data is irretrievable.、「データを定期的にバックアップします」は、I back up the data periodically. と言う。

chapter 1 Working at the Office

49 メールサーバーがダウンして、一時はどうなることかと思った。
When the mail server was down, I had no idea what would happen.

50 あんな長いネイルでよくあんなに速くタイプできるなぁ。
Look how fast she can type with such long nails!

51 キーボードのたたきすぎで肩がガチガチにこってきた。
Hammering at the keys is giving me stiff shoulders.

52 いったい、どれだけアナログ人間なんですか!
How out of touch are you?

53 PCがトラブるたびに呼ばないで。私はあなたのヘルプデスクじゃない!
Please don't ask me for help every time something's wrong with your computer. I'm not your helpdesk.

have no idea = 全くわからない

「(どうして良いかわからず) 途方に暮れる」を意味する表現には find oneself in a stew (シチューの中にいるような気分) もある。e.g. He found himself in a stew because no one showed up at his presentation. (誰もプレゼンに来なかったので彼は途方に暮れた)

Look how fast ~! = ほら、なんて速く~なんだろう!

「タイプするのがうまい」は type well、「両手 (10本の指) を使ってタイプする」は type with all one's fingers、「キーボードを見ないでタイプ (ブラインドタッチ) する」は type without looking at the keyboard、もしくは touch-type と言う。

---

hammer at ~ = [ハンマーで打ち込むように激しく]~をたたく／stiff shoulders = 肩こり

「慢性的な肩こり」は chronic stiff shoulders と言う。I see a masseuse to ease my stiff shoulders. で「肩こり解消のためにマッサージに通っています」。

---

out of touch = 疎い、無関心な

out of touch は「接触していない」、つまり「[世間に] 無関心な」の意味なので、PC関連以外の話題でももちろん使える。e.g. I'm out of touch with the latest information, so please help me catch up/fill me in. (最新情報に疎いので、話を聞かせてください)

---

ask ~ for help = ~に助けを求める／helpdesk = ヘルプデスク

I call the helpdesk to fix my computer. で「パソコンを修理してもらうためにヘルプデスクに電話する」。「便利屋、雑用係」は handyman と言う。e.g. I don't want to be called a handyman. (何でも屋って呼ばれたくないなあ)

Skit 内勤編

もしもIT人間が一般事務を手伝ったら……

Woman: This can't be happening! I've got a computer virus.
Man: Don't panic①. I'll take a look at② it.
W: Oh, I've got more work than I can manage already. I still have to answer the phone and send a fax.
M: Can I help with③ something?
W: Will you make 10 copies of the financial statements for the first quarter?
M: You're kidding! The copier gets jammed every time I use scrap paper.
W: Then don't use scrap paper.
M: Ha, ha, ha. Very funny.
W: Just clip the documents together for the meeting at 4 o'clock.
M: I don't know where the paper clips are.
W: How out of touch are you④?
M: Hey, I'm good at⑤ computers. I can reboot your computer, set up the printer and set your password, but I don't know much about general office work⑥.
W: All right. You deal with⑦ the computer. I'll make the copies.

女性：まさか！ ウイルスに感染しちゃった。
男性：あわてないで。僕が見てあげるから。
女：もう、仕事がキャパを超えちゃってるのよ！ 電話取ったりファクス送ったりするのも私の仕事だし。
男：何か手伝おうか。
女：第一四半期の決算資料のコピーを10部ずつ取ってくれる？
男：うそ〜。このコピー、裏紙使うたびに紙づまりしちゃうんだよ〜。
女：じゃ、裏紙使わないで。
男：はははは。面白いこと言うねえ。
女：4時の会議用に書類をクリップでまとめてくれるだけでいいわ。
男：クリップ、どこにあるんだろ。
女：ほんと、どれだけ物を知らないの？
男：あのさあ、僕はコンピューターには強いんだよ。君のパソコンの再起動とか、プリンターのセッティングとか、パスワードの設定もしてあげられるよ。でも、一般事務のことはあまり知らないんだ。
女：わかったわよ。あなたはパソコンのことやって。コピーは私が取るから。

【語注】
❶panic: あわてる、パニックに陥る
❷take a look at ~: ~を調べる、見る
❸help with ~: ~について助ける
❹How out of touch are you ?: ここではp.38の㊼とは正反対の文脈で、文字どおり「どれだけ物を知らないのか？」の意味で使われている。
❺be good at ~: ~が上手だ、得意だ
❻general office work: 一般的な事務の仕事
❼deal with ~: ~を扱う

Quick Check

本章に出てきたフレーズを復習しましょう。以下の日本語の意味になるよう英文を完成させてください。答えはページの下にあります。

❶電話を保留にする。 ➡P016
I ( ) the call ( ) ( ).

❷仕事の流れを把握する。 ➡P016
I ( ) ( ) of the ( ).

❸業務の見直しをして、無駄な作業を省く。 ➡P017
I ( ) the ( ) to ( ) ( ) jobs.

❹書類に上司のサインをもらう。 ➡P017
I ( ) my boss ( ) the documents.

❺小口現金の管理をする。 ➡P018
I ( ) ( ) ( ) the ( ) cash.

❻ギリギリセーフ！ 間に合った！ ➡P022
I ( ) ( )! ( ) ( ) ( ) for work!

❼引き出しが古い資料でパンパン。そろそろ整理しなきゃ。 ➡P022
My drawers are ( ) ( ) ( ) ( ) old papers.
Guess ( ) ( ) ( ) ( ) them.

❽書類が溜まっているから今日は腰をすえて一日社内で事務仕事だ。 ➡P022
( ) all the documents that have ( ) ( ), I have to
( ) ( ) ( ) office work all day today.

❾最近クレーム続きだから電話を取るのもドキドキだよ。 ➡P026
Since we've been having a lot of customer ( ) recently, just ( )
( ) the phone ( ) me ( ) in ( ) ( ).

❿キーボードのたたきすぎで肩がガチガチにこってきた。 ➡P038
( ) ( ) the ( ) is ( ) me ( ) ( ).

---

❶put/on/hold ❷make/sure/workflow ❸review/workflow/eliminate/unnecessary ❹have/sign ❺keep/track/of/petty ❻made/it/Just/in/time ❼filled/to/capacity/with/it's/time/to/organize ❽With/piled/up/buckle/down/to ❾complaints/picking/up/gives/butterflies/my/stomach ❿Hammering/at/keys/giving/stiff/shoulders

42

chapter 2

人間関係
Human Relationships

上司、同僚、先輩、後輩——
オフィスライフを送る上で
避けて通れないのが職場の人間関係。
教えたり教えられたり、
面倒を掛けたり掛けられたりする中で
思わずひとりごちる機会も多そうです。

chapter 2 Human Relationships

Words 単語編

❸ 係長、課長
❹ 課長代理
❺ 課長、部長
❻ 部長、幹部
❼ 管理職
❽ 中間管理職
❾ 同僚
❿ 同期、仲間
⓫ 社内恋愛
⓬ 職場結婚
❶ 新人
❷ 助手

❶ new employee/[new] recruit/rookie ❷ assistant ❸ chief
❹ deputy general manager ❺ [general] manager ❻ [general] director ❼ management ❽ middle management ❾ colleague/co-worker ❿ peer ⓫ office romance ⓬ marriage between

まずは、さまざまな物や事の名前で
「人間関係」のシーンのイメージをつかもう。

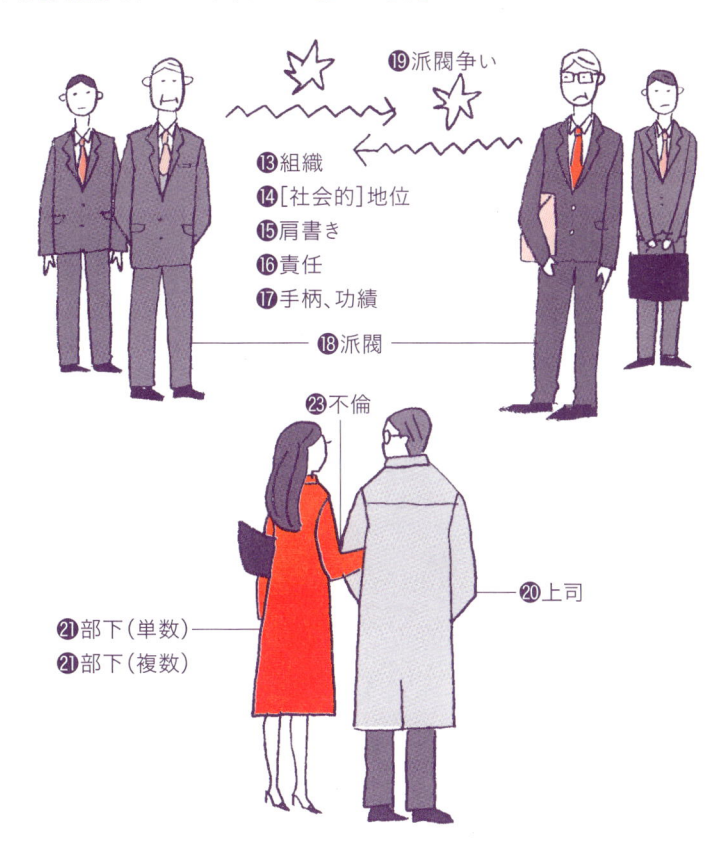

⑲派閥争い
⑬組織
⑭[社会的]地位
⑮肩書き
⑯責任
⑰手柄、功績
⑱派閥
㉓不倫
⑳上司
㉑部下(単数)
㉑部下(複数)

co-workers ⑬organization ⑭position ⑮title ⑯responsibility
⑰credit ⑱faction ⑲factional fighting ⑳boss/supervisor/
superior ㉑staff member/subordinate ㉒staff ㉓[extramarital]
affair

chapter 2 Human Relationships

1 上司に指示を仰ぐ
I ask my boss for instructions.

2 上司に個人的な相談に乗ってもらう
I ask my boss for advice on personal matters.

3 上司に仕事の不満を訴える
I complain to my boss about my job.

4 上司にたてつく
I talk back to my boss.

5 上司のご機嫌取りをする
I butter up my boss.

tips

❶ ask ~ for ... は「〜に…を求める」。
❷ personal matters（個人的な事柄）は personal stuff でも同じ。
❸ complain は「不満、不平を言う」。
❺ butter up は「ご機嫌を取る」。「上司を喜ばせようとする」なら I try to please my boss / make my boss feel better. としてもよい。

6 上司のグチに付き合わされる
I endure listening to my boss's complaints.

7 同僚とうまくやっていく
I get along well with my <u>colleagues/co-workers</u>.

8 同僚の一人と気まずくなる
I begin to feel uneasy with one of my <u>colleagues/co-workers</u>.

9 同僚に成績で差をつけられる
I was left behind by my <u>co-workers/colleagues</u> in business performance.

10 同僚の尻ぬぐいをする
I clear up my co-worker's mess.

❻ I have to listen to my boss <u>complain/grumble</u>. でも同じ意味。
❽ feel uneasy は「落ち着かない、気兼ねする」。I find it difficult to get along with one of my co-workers. でもよい。
❿「同僚のミスを埋め合わせなくては(正さなくては)ならない」I have to <u>cover</u>(<u>straighten out</u>) my co-worker's mistakes. と言い換えられる。

chapter ❷ Human Relationships

11 新人に仕事を教える
I explain the job to the new employee.

12 部下をマンツーマンで指導する
I instruct my staff member one on one.

13 部下に指示する
I give instructions to my staff member.

14 後輩に仕事を引き継ぐ
I have my younger colleague take over my job.

15 部下に一任する
I leave the job to my staff member.

tips

⓫ I instruct the [new] recruit about the job procedures. でも同じ。
⓬「マンツーマン」はone on one(一対一)の表現が一般的。「部下」一人の場合はa staff memberで、staffは「部下たち」。
⓭ I tell my staff member what to do.(部下に何をするか指示する)と言ってもよい。

16 部下にやる気を出させる
I try to motivate my staff.

17 部下を褒める(しかる)
I <u>praise</u>(<u>reprimand</u>) my staff member.

18 部下たちの肩を持つ(支持する)
I <u>take my staff's side</u>(<u>back up</u> / <u>stick up for</u> my staff).

19 部下をえこひいきする
I favor one of my staff over everyone else.

20 部下に花を持たせる
I let my staff member take the credit.

⑯ motivate は「やる気にさせる、モチベーションを与える」。
⑰ 厳しく「しかる」なら rebuke (強く非難する)を使う。「しかる」に scold を使うと、相手が子どもであるような印象を与える。
⑲ 「特別扱いする」は I give one staff member special treatment.。

chapter ❷ Human Relationships

21 従業員の悩みを聞く
I listen to my employee talk about the <u>problems/worries</u> [she has].

22 積極的に社内交流する
I actively try to get to know the people in the company.

23 社内で趣味のネットワークを作る
I build a network of co-workers who have the same interests.

24 同僚と職場恋愛(結婚)する
I get <u>involved with (married to)</u> my colleague.

25 上司と不倫をする
I have an affair with my boss.

tips
㉑ problem は「問題」、worry は「心配、悩みの種」。
㉒「交流する」は know の代わりに meet や interact with を使ってもよい。
㉓「同じ趣味の同僚」co-workers with the same interests でも可。
㉔「同僚に恋する」は I have fallen in love with my colleague.、「同僚と結婚する」は I marry my colleague.。

会社組織関連語

株主 **stockholder**　　株主総会 **stockholders' meeting**

幹部、責任者

最高経営責任者 **CEO**(Chief Executive Officer)
最高財務責任者 **CFO**(Chief Financial Officer)
最高業務責任者 **COO**(Chief Operating Officer)
代表取締役 **representative director**
会長 **chairperson**
社長 **president**
副社長 **vice president**
専務 **senior managing director**
常務 **executive managing director**
役員、幹部 **executive**(exec)
取締役会、重役会 **Board of Directors**
事業本部 **Operational Headquarters**(OHQ)
部長、幹部 **[general] director**
部長、課長 **[general] manager**
課長、係長 **chief**

監査部 **audit department**
監査人 **auditor**
会計監査人 **controller**

秘書室 **Office of Secretariat**
秘書 **secretary**

部、部門 Department(Dept.) 部局 Division

総務部 **general affairs** ～
経理部 **accounting** ～
財務部 **finance** ～
法務部 **legal** ～
人事部
　personnel/**human resources** ～
企画部 **planning** ～
研究開発部
　research & development ～
営業部 **sales** ～
システム部 **system** ～
広報部 **public relations** ～
製造部 **manufacturing** ～
物流部 **logistics** ～

課 Section

販売促進課 **sales promotion** ～
商品開発課 **product planning** ～
生産管理課 **product control** ～
品質管理課 **quality control** ～

chapter ❷ Human Relationships

1. 人間関係(上司)に恵まれてるなあ。
I'm really lucky to have <u>good personal relationships</u>(<u>a good boss</u>) at work.

2. 彼には借りがあるから断れないや。
I owe him <u>a favor</u> / <u>a lot</u>, so I can't say no to him.

3. どうもあの人苦手だなあ。
I find it hard to get along with that person.

4. 隣にいるのに何でもメールで連絡するのってよそよそしいよね。
I think it's very unfriendly to use e-mail for everything, especially when the person is sitting right next to you.

5. 職場の人とは距離を置いて付き合いたい。
I try not to get too personal with my co-workers.

6. 派閥争いには巻き込まれたくないなあ。
I don't want to get <u>involved</u> / <u>caught up</u> in the factional fighting.

lucky = 運がいい／**personal relationships** = 人間関係／**at work** = 仕事で cf. in the officeと言ってもよい

逆に「会社での人間関係がよくない」と言うなら I'm not happy with the personal relationships in the office.。

---

owe = 借りがある、おかげである cf. I owe a lot to you. = あなたには大変お世話になっています。／**favor** = 親切な行為、世話／**say no** = ノーと言う、断る

「断れない」は turn down（断る、退ける）を使って I can't turn him down. と言ってもよい。

---

find it hard to ~ = ~するのは難しいと思う（この場合のfindは「気づく、~だと感じる」）／**get along with ~** = と付き合う、うまくやっていく

相手をするのが難しい人の場合は That person is difficult/tough to deal with. と言うこともできる。

---

unfriendly = そっけない、無愛想な cf. unsociable = 非社交的な／**for everything** = あらゆることに／**especially** = とりわけ／**sit right next to ~** = ~のすぐ隣に座る

Don't you think it's rather unsociable when the person sitting next to you uses e-mail to contact you for everything? と疑問形にしてもよい。

---

too~ = あまりにも~な／**personal** = 個人的な、私的な／**co-worker** = 同僚 cf. colleague でも同じ

「距離 (distance) を置いていたい」をそのまま使って I like to keep my distance with co-workers. と言ってもよい。

---

get involved in ~ = ~に巻き込まれる、かかわり合いになる／**get caught up in ~** = ~に巻き込まれる（caughtはcatchの過去・過去分詞形）／**factional fighting** = 派閥争い cf. faction = 派閥、党派

「否応なしに派閥争いに巻き込まれた」は I was forced to be involved in the factional fighting.。

chapter 2 Human Relationships

7 頑張れ、わたし！
Come on! I can do it!

8 あんなデキる上司の下で働きたいなあ。
<u>I wish I could</u> / <u>I really want to</u> work for such a competent boss.

9 福岡部長には、一生ついていきたい。
I'd like to work with our manager, Ms. Fukuoka, throughout my career!

10 うちの上司は面倒見がよくて慕われている。
My boss takes good care of people and so she is respected [by them].

11 彼は部下をやる気にさせるのがうまい。
He really knows how to motivate his <u>staff</u>/<u>people</u>.

12 部長は何も見てないようで、実は結構細かいところをチェックしてるんだよね。
The manager never seems to notice anything, but actually he is checking the details [<u>closely</u>/<u>carefully</u>].

I can do it = 自分はできる

「頑張れ！」は Come on! のほかに Don't give up!（あきらめるな）、Go for it!（行け！）、Keep it up!（この調子で頑張れ）などさまざまな表現がある。

I wish I could ~ = ~できたらいいのに（控えめな願望を表す表現）／work for ~ = ~のために働く／such a ~ = こんな／competent = 有能な、仕事ができる

「彼は仕事が<u>できる</u>／<u>できない</u>」は He is <u>competent</u>/<u>incompetent</u> at work.。

---

work with ~ = ~と共に仕事をする／throughout ~ = ~を通してずっと cf. throughout life = 一生を通じて／**career[kəríər] = [一生の]職業、仕事（発音に注意）**

「一生」は throughout my career の代わりに「ずっと」forever と言ってもよい。

---

take care of ~ = ~の面倒を見る／be respected by ~ = ~から尊敬されている cf. respect = 尊敬する

後半は so everyone likes her としてもよい。主語を we に変えると We <u>respect</u>/<u>like</u> our boss because she takes good care of people.（面倒見がいいので私たちは上司を慕っている）となる。

---

how to ~ = ~するやり方、方法／motivate = やる気にさせる cf. motivation = やる気、意欲、モチベーション／**staff = 部下たち**

「やる気が出る」は I <u>feel</u>/<u>am</u> really motivated.、逆に「やる気がなくなった」なら I've lost my motivation.。

---

notice = 気がつく／actually = 実は、本当は／detail = 細かい部分、詳細 cf. in detail = 詳しく、詳細に／**closely = 念入りに、詳しく／carefully = 注意深く、じっくりと**

「細かいところまで詳しく話してください」は Could you tell me about it in detail?。命令口調で Tell me about it right down to the smallest detail. という言い方もある。

chapter 2 Human Relationships

13 親父ギャグさえ言わなければいい上司なんだけど。
He is a good boss except for his lame jokes.

14 あんな人使いの荒い上司は初めてだ。もっと部下を思いやって欲しいよ。
I've never worked for a boss who pushed us so hard. She should be more considerate of the staff.

15 理不尽に部下を怒鳴りつけるなんて、パワハラだよね。
I think it's "power harassment" to yell at your staff without any good reason.

16 ちぇっ。何もみんなの前であんなふうに言わなくたっていいじゃないか。
Tsk! He shouldn't have spoken in that way in front of everyone!

17 今朝は部長、機嫌が悪そうだなぁ。
The manager seems to be in a bad mood this morning.

18 気分屋の上司は勘弁。
I don't want to have a boss who is moody. Give me a break!

except for~ = ～以外は、～がなかったら／lame joke = つまらない冗談
cf.lame = 説得力のない、下手な、まずい
gag は「漫才や喜劇でのギャグ」なので joke が無難。「親父ギャグ」は an old man's joke と直訳しても通じない。「駄じゃれ」は pun と言う。

I've never ~ = 一度も～したことがない／push ~ hard = ～に無理をさせる、人使いが荒い／be considerate of ~ = ～に気をつかう、思いやりがある
後半は She should treat us more kindly.（もっと優しく接してほしい）と言い換えられる。

---

power harassment = パワハラ　cf. harassment = 嫌がらせ、迷惑／yell = 怒鳴る／without any good reason = もっともな理由なしに
power harassment は元々和製英語であるが、現在では *karoshi* などと同様、労働環境に関する用語として海外で使われることもある。「セクハラ」は sexual harassment。英語では harassment は短縮できない。

---

tsk = ちぇっ(舌打ちの音)／shouldn't have ~ = ～すべきではなかった(過去にやったことに対して)／in that way = あのように、あんなふうに
He shouldn't have said something like that in front of everybody!（皆の前であんなことを言わなくても！）でも同じ。

---

seem to be ~ = ～のように見える／in a bad mood = 不機嫌　cf. mood = 気分、機嫌（文脈によってはmoodだけで「不機嫌」という意味にもなる）
in a bad mood の代わりに grumpy（機嫌の悪い、イライラした）を使ってもよい。

---

moody = 気分の変わりやすい、気分屋の／Give me a break! = 勘弁して! いいかげんにしてくれ!(くだけた言い方) cf. break = 中断、途切れ、休み
「勘弁して！」はほかに Come on!、Not again!（もう二度とだめな場合に使う）など。

chapter 2 Human Relationships

19 部長、むかつく!
My boss gets on my nerves!

20 上司が何だ!
To hell with the boss!

21 決断できずに逃げてばかりの上司にはうんざり。
I'm <u>tired</u>/<u>sick</u> of having a boss who can't make a decision and always avoids responsibility.

22 部下に丸投げされても困るんだよなあ。
I'm at a loss when the boss leaves all the decision-making to us.

23 任せると言っておいて、最後の最後にダメ出し?!
[It's <u>unbelievable</u>/<u>impossible</u>!] He left everything to me and then disapproved at the last minute!

24 上司に手柄を横取りされた。
My boss took all the credit for my work.

get on one's nerves = 神経に障る、イライラさせる／**nerves** = 神経過敏、イライラ cf. nerve = 神経、度胸 | He's got a real nerve! = 彼は本当に図々しい

「むかつく」は俗語表現では I get pissed off!、もう少しおとなしい表現なら I'm upset.（腹が立つ）と言う。

To hell with ~ = ~が何だ、~はうんざりだ（くだけた言い方。**The hell with ~** も同じ）／**hell** = 地獄、ひどいこと cf. like hell = ひどく、必死に

罵り言葉は相手や状況を考えて注意して使うこと。Go to hell!（地獄に落ちろ！、くたばれ！）はかなり下品な罵り言葉。

---

be tired of ~ = ~にはうんざりだ cf. sick of ~ も同じ／**make a decision** = 決定する、決断を下す／**avoid** = ~を避ける／**responsibility** = 責任　cf. take responsibility = 責任を取る

「決断できない上司」は boss who can't make up his mind とも言える。

---

at a loss = 困って、途方に暮れて／**leave ~ to ...** = ~を[人]任せにする／**decision-making** = 意思決定

I'm at a loss の代わりに I don't know what to do（どうしていいかわからない）と言ってもよい。

---

unbelievable = 信じられない／**impossible** = 不可能だ、ありえない／**disapprove** = 反対する、不可とする cf. approve = 承認する、認める／**at the last minute** = 間際になって、最後の最後で

「あなたに任せます」は I'll leave it to you.、「私に任せて！」なら Just leave it to me! となる。

---

take credit for ~ = ~を自分の手柄にする、~を横取りする cf. credit = 手柄、功績

「手柄が欲しくて仕事をしているわけではない」と言うのなら I'm not doing my job to get credit.。

chapter 2 Human Relationships

25 彼、佐川部長といつももめすぎ。
He's always arguing too much with the manager, Mr. Sagawa.

26 上と下との板ばさみで、中間管理職ってほんとつらい。
It's very hard to be in middle management because you're always stuck in the middle.

27 部下を持ってわかる、上司の苦労。
I understood the difficulty of being in charge [for the first time] when I had someone working under me.

28 上司の居ぬ間に洗濯。
Let's have fun while the boss is away!

29 やっと後輩ができた！ ペーペー卒業だ！
Finally, I have a colleague younger than me! I'm no longer the youngest worker here.

30 新人って初々しくていいなあ。
The new <u>employees</u>/<u>recruits</u> seem so young and fresh.

argue with ~ = ～と口論する、言い争う、議論する cf. argue about ~ = ～について議論する

He's having a <u>fight</u>/<u>trouble</u> with the manager again.（彼、また部長とけんかして／もめている）とも言える。

---

middle management = 中間管理職 cf. management = 管理職／**stuck = 動けない、はまり込んだ（stuckはstickの過去・過去分詞形）／in the middle = 真ん中に**

「中間管理職は上役と部下の間で板ばさみになっている」は The middle manager is caught between superiors and subordinates.。

---

difficulty of ~ = ～の難しさ、困難／be in charge = 責任者になる／for the first time = 初めて／work under ~ = ～の下で働く、～の部下となって働く

「上司の苦労なんて考えたこともなかった」と言うなら I never thought about what my boss went through.。

---

have fun = 楽しむ／while ~ = ～する間に／away = 不在で、いない

Let's relax while the boss is out! と言い換えられる。ことわざの「鬼の居ぬ間に洗濯」は英語では When the cat's away, the mice will play.（猫がいない間にネズミが遊ぶ）。

---

finally = ついに、とうとう／no longer = もはや～でない

「まだペーペーだ」は I'm still at the bottom of the <u>hierarchy</u>/<u>ladder</u>.（序列の一番下）と言う。「平社員」は <u>an ordinary</u> ／ <u>a rank-and-file</u> employee。

---

fresh = 新鮮な、新しい、新米の cf. a person fresh out of college = 大学出たての若者、大学出たてのホヤホヤ

「新人はまだ未熟（経験不足）だね」は The new employees are still wet behind the ears. だが、これにはネガティブなニュアンスがある。

chapter 2 Human Relationships

31 新人の教育係は彼女が適任だと思う。
I think she is the right person to train the new employees.

32 私は褒められて伸びるタイプなんです！
I'm the type of person who will get better by being praised.

33 彼は言われたことしかやらないんだよなあ。
He does only what he is told [and nothing else].

34 後輩が生意気で気に入らない。
One of my younger colleagues gets on my nerves because she is so defiant!

35 ちょっと、新人。足、引っ張らないで！
Hey, rookie! Don't get in my way!

36 新人いびりじゃない、指導してるだけだよ。
I'm not picking on the new employees, just giving them guidance.

the right person to ~ = ~するのにふさわしい人 cf. right = 適切な、ちょうど良い／**train = 訓練する**

「私には適任じゃない（できない、気が向かない）」と言うなら I'm not up to it.。

---

the type of person who ~ = ~というタイプの人間／get better = 良くなる、上達する／praise = ほめる、称賛する cf. 名詞は「称賛、褒め言葉」

I'm the kind of person who will thrive on praise.（褒め言葉で育つ人間だ）でも同じ意味。thrive は「成長する、育つ」。

---

what he is told = 言われたこと cf. do what one is told = 言われたことをやる／**nothing else = 他に何も[しない]**

He doesn't do anything unless he is told to do it.（彼は言われないと何もしない）と言うこともできる。

---

younger colleague = 若い同僚（英語では会社の「後輩」に当てはまる言い方はない）／**get on one's nerves = イライラさせる／defiant = 反抗的な** cf. ほかに cheeky（生意気な）、arrogant（傲慢な）、rude（無礼な）、a smart-alec[k]（生意気な人）などと言い換えられる

I don't like one of my younger colleagues because she thinks she is so smart!（あの後輩は自分がすごく賢いと思っているから嫌）とも。

---

rookie = 新人、ルーキー cf. rookieの代わりに new guy/girlと呼び掛けることもできる／**get in one's way = ~の邪魔をする、~の足を引っ張る**

後半は Don't cause any trouble!（迷惑をかけないで！）と言い換えてもよい。

---

pick on = いじめる、いびる／new employee = 新入社員／guidance = 指導

I'm not being mean to the new employees, only instructing them. と言っても同じ意味。mean は「意地悪な」。

chapter ❷ Human Relationships

37 若いうちは文句言ってるだけでいいからいい気なもんだ。
When you are young, you just complain [and do nothing]. You think you can get away with anything!

38 あの子はいつも明るくて仕事頼みやすいんだよね。
She is always cheerful so you can easily ask her to do a job.

39 彼女は職場のムードメーカーだ。
She brightens up the office.

40 彼ってさりげなく気配りができる人だよね。
He can be attentive in a very subtle way.

41 伊藤さんは職場で頼れる存在だ。
Ms. Ito is someone we can count on in the office.

42 彼って公私共に非の打ち所がないよね！
He is a perfect guy both personally and professionally!

complain = 不満を言う、文句を言う／**do nothing** = 何もしない／**get away with ~** = ~をうまく逃れる、やり過ごす cf. get away with doing nothing = 何もせずにその場を切り抜ける

「何をしても許されると思ったら大間違いだ」と言うなら If you think you can get away with anything, you are wrong.

---

cheerful = 快活な、朗らかな／**easily** = 気楽に、簡単に

She is such a cheerful person that you never mind asking her to do something.（彼女はとても明るいので、気にせずに仕事を頼める）と言い換えても同じ意味。

---

brighten up ~ = ~を活気づける、明るくする cf. bright = 明るい、快活な

She cheers everyone up.（皆を元気づける）、She makes everyone feel happy in the office.（会社の皆を楽しい気持ちにさせる）と言い換えることができる。（×）moodmaker は和製英語なので使えない。

---

attentive = [人を]気遣う、[人に]思いやりのある／**in a subtle way** = それとなく cf. subtle = かすかな、繊細な（発音に注意[sʌ́tl]）

He is considerate/thoughtful in a very casual way. とも言える。considerate は「よく気が利く」、thoughtful は「思いやりのある」。

---

someone we can ~ = われわれが~できる人／**count on** = ~を頼りにする、~を当てにする cf. rely on と言ってもよい

in the office の代わりに at work と言ってもよい。「あなたはいつも頼りになる」なら I can always count on you.。

---

perfect = 非の打ちどころがない、完全な／**both A and B** = AもBも両方／**professionally** = 職業上

He is a perfect guy の代わりに He is perfect でも同じ。「公私の区別をつける」は draw a line between public/professional and private/personal lives と言う。draw a line between ~ and ... で「~と…の間に線引きする」。

chapter 2 Human Relationships

43 彼は上にはゴマするけど、下には冷たい。
He always kisses up to his superiors but is very cold to his subordinates.

---

44 彼、仕事ではいいけど個人的には付き合いたくない人だよ。
He's OK to work with, but I don't want to deal with him personally.

---

45 この会社、職場結婚がすごく多いよね。
Don't you think we have a lot of marriages between co-workers at this company?

---

46 同期で結婚してないの、自分だけだ!
I'm the only one who is not married among my peers!

---

47 寿退社ってやっぱり憧れるよね。
I've always wanted to get married and leave the company.

---

48 いまどき社内恋愛禁止ってどうなの?
I can't believe they still forbid office romance.

kiss up to ~ = ~にへつらう cf.「ゴマをする」はほかにbutter up（機嫌を取る）、flatter（お世辞を言う）、suck up（おべっかを使う）などで言い換え可能／**superior** = 上司／**subordinate** = 部下

「嫌いな相手でもゴマをするような人は信用できない」なら、I can't trust people who butter up someone they don't like. と言える。

---

work with ~ = ~と一緒に働く／**deal with ~** = ~を相手にする、~に対応する／**personally** = 個人的に

後半は I don't want to get involved with him personally.、または I don't want to be friends with him. と言ってもよい。get involved with ~ は「~とかかわり合う」、be friends with ~ は「~と友達づきあいする」。

Don't you think~? = ~だと思わない？（同意を求める表現）／**marriage between ~** = ~の間の結婚 cf. get married to a co-worker = 同僚と結婚する

So many people have gotten married to co-workers at our company.（この会社ではとても多くの同僚同士が結婚している）と言い換えられる。

---

the only one = 唯一の人／**be married** = 結婚している／**among ~** = ~の間で／**peer** = 仲間、同僚、同輩

I'm the only girl/guy my age at work who isn't married.（会社で自分はこの年齢で結婚していないただ一人の女性／男性だ）と言ってもよい。

I've always wanted to ~ = ずっと~してみたいと思っていた／**get married** = 結婚する／**leave the company** = 退社する、退職する

I wish I could get married and quit my job.（結婚して仕事を辞められたらいいのに）とも言える。

I can't believe = 信じられない／**forbid** = ~を禁止する、許さない／**office romance** = 職場・社内恋愛 cf. have an office romance = 職場恋愛をする

office romance の部分を workers to get involved in a relationship（社員が恋愛関係を持つこと）と言い換えても通じる。

ビジネスシーンに必要なマナー&表現

　国や文化によって違いはあるが、ビジネスの場面での会話では基本的にフォーマルな表現やマナーを心掛けておけば間違いないだろう。

1. フォーマルな場面での出会い

　フォーマルな場面で出会った**初対面の相手**には、"(It's) nice to meet you."、"I'm <u>pleased</u>/<u>very glad</u> to meet you."（お会いできてうれしいです）などとあいさつをしよう。相手と握手をする場合は相手の顔（目）を見ながら、しっかりと手を握ること。特にアメリカでは、男性同士が握手するときに弱々しい握手では相手から信頼されない。なお、名刺交換(exchanging business cards)は欧米では一般的ではなく、こういった日本の習慣は通じない可能性もあるから注意が必要だ。

　自己紹介するときには、"<u>I am</u>/<u>My name is</u> Akiko Okada."（岡田明子です）とフルネームで自分の名前を言おう。勤務先などについては "I work for A Company."（A社に勤めています）、"I work in the <u>sales</u>(<u>accounting</u>) department."「営業（経理）部で働いています」と言えばよい。

　相手に呼び掛ける場合には、敬称(Mr./Ms.)をラストネーム（名字）につける(例：Mr. Hayashi、Ms. Okada)のが普通である。親しい間柄でカジュアルな場面なら、下の名前、ファーストネーム（例：Kohei、Akiko）を使うこともある。特にアメリカでは、気軽にファーストネームで呼び合うことが多い。このとき、ファーストネームには敬称をつけないように気をつけよう(×Mr. Alan、×Ms. Audrey)。なお、上司に対して、日本語では「課長」、「部長」のように呼び掛けるが、英語では役職名ではなく、その人の名字を敬称付きで呼ぶ(Mr. Spader、Ms. Schmidt)のが一般的である。

2. 言葉を交わすときのマナーや丁寧表現

　次に、相手と話すときには、**アイコンタクト**（相手の目を見ること）を意識しよう。

荒井 貴和　Text by Kiwa Arai

適切なところで**相槌をうつ**ことも必要だ。ただし、日本語の「ええ」のつもりで"Yes"と言うと、相手の話の内容に同意している("Yes, I agree.")という意味になり、誤解を招くことがある。意味的に中立な相槌（uh-huh、I seeなど）を使う方が無難。

　英語には、日本語の敬語そのものにあたるものはないが、敬意を表す表現、つまり丁寧な言い方はある。まず代表的なのが、would、could、may、mightなどの**助動詞を使った丁寧な表現**。例えば、相手に何かを頼む場合、命令文にpleaseをつけただけでは横柄な印象を与えることがある（"Answer the phone, please!"「電話に出て！」）。カジュアルな場面なら"Can you answer the phone?"（電話に出てくれる？）と言えばいいが、もっと丁寧に言いたいならWould/Could you ~? を使って表すことができる（"Could you answer the phone?"＜電話に出ていただけませんか＞）。

　また、自分が何かしたい場合には、I'd/We'd like to ~（~したいと思っています）という表現を覚えておくと、幅広く使えてとても便利である。例えばWe'd like to do a questionnaire.（アンケートを実施したいと思っております）のように言える。本書に出てくるさまざまな表現を入れて使ってみよう。

　ほかに"Do you mind ~?"（~してもかまいませんか？）や、"I'm afraid ~"（あいにくですが~）、"if I may"（もしよろしければ）なども丁寧な表現としてさまざまな場面で活用できるので、ぜひ覚えて使ってほしい。

　なお、カジュアルな会話では、省略やくだけた言い方(例："I wanna~"、"I'm gonna~"、"kinda"、"Yeah"、"Thanks!"など)をよく使うが、フォーマルな場合には**できるだけ省略せずにきちんとした言い方**を心掛けたい（"I want to~"、I'm going to ~"、"kind of ~"、"Yes"、"Thank you."）。また、カジュアルな場面なら俗語的表現や罵り言葉もある程度許される場合もあるが、ビジネスの場面ではこれらは避けるべきである。

Skit 人間関係編

中間管理職、ぼやきの種は尽きまじ

Man: **I wish I could work for such a competent boss. You're lucky.**

Woman: **He takes good care of people, so we respect him He's a good boss except for his lame jokes.**

M: **My boss gets on my nerves. I have to endure listening to his complaints. He can't make decisions and always avoids responsibility. But he can be attentive in a very subtle way.**

W: **Well, at least**① **you really know how to motivate your people.**

M: **I try. I praise them and stick up for them, and I let them take credit for what they do.**

W: **It's hard to be in middle management because we're always stuck in the middle.**

M: **Don't give up. We can do it.**

男性：僕もあんなできる上司の下で働きたいなあ。君がうらやましいよ。
女性：彼は面倒見が良くて、みんなに慕われてるの。あの親父ギャグさえなかったら、本当にいい上司よ。
男：僕の上司、頭にくるんだ。愚痴には付き合わされるし、決断できずに逃げてばかり。ただ、妙にさりげなく気を遣ってくれたりはするんだけど。
女：でもまあ、少なくともあなたは自分の部下にやる気を起こさせるすべを知ってるわよね。
男：努力はしてるよ。褒めたり応援したり、仕事を認めて花を持たせてやったり。
女：上と下との板挟みで、中間管理職ってつらいわよねえ。
男：頑張ろう！ 僕らならできるよ。

【語注】

❶ at least: 少なくとも

Quick Check

本章に出てきたフレーズを復習しましょう。以下の日本語の意味になるよう
英文を完成させてください。答えはページの下にあります。

❶上司のご機嫌取りをする。 ➡P046
I ( ) ( ) my boss.

❷同僚に成績で差をつけられる。 ➡P047
I was ( ) ( ) by my colleagues/co-workers in ( )
( )

❸後輩に仕事を引き継ぐ。 ➡P048
I have my younger colleague ( ) ( ) my job.

❹彼には借りがあるから断れないや。 ➡P052
I ( ) him a ( ), so I can't ( ) ( ) to him.

❺どうもあの人苦手だなあ。 ➡P052
I ( ) ( ) ( ) ( ) ( ) ( )
( ) that person.

❻派閥争いには巻き込まれたくないなあ。 ➡P052
I don't want to ( ) ( ) ( ) the ( ) ( ).

❼気分屋の上司は勘弁。 ➡P056
I don't want to have a boss who is ( ). ( ) ( )
( ) ( )!

❽部下に丸投げされても困るんだよなあ。 ➡P058
I'm ( ) ( ) ( ) when the boss ( ) all the
( ) to us.

❾ちょっと、新人。足、引っ張らないで！ ➡P062
Hey, ( )! Don't ( ) ( ) ( ) ( )!

❿彼女は職場のムードメーカーだ。 ➡P064
She ( ) ( ) the office.

---

❶butter/up ❷left/behind/business / performance ❸take/over ❹owe/favor or lot/say/no ❺find/it/hard/to/get/along/with ❻get/involved/in/factional fighting ❼moody/ Give/me/a/break ❽at/a/loss/leaves/decision-making ❾rookie/get/in/my/way ❿brightens/up

chapter 3
営業
Salesperson

会社の命運(利益)を背負って立つ
営業パーソンにまつわる表現です。
外回り営業で、商品やサービスについて
顧客に説明したり交渉したりして
数字達成を目指す人々の、ちょっと
気合いの入った行動やつぶやきの数々。

chapter 3 Salesperson

Words 単語編

❶営業マン
❷外回り
❸飛び込み営業
❹ルート営業
❺顧客
❻担当者
❼名刺
❽第一印象
❾営業トーク
❿世間話
⓫営業スマイル

❶salesperson ❷sales round ❸walk-in sales ❹regular sales ❺customer/client ❻person in charge ❼business card ❽first impression ❾sales talk ❿small talk ⓫business smile ⓬seat

まずは、さまざまな物や事の名前で
「営業」のシーンのイメージをつかもう。

㉓営業成績
⑳売上記録
㉑目標数値
㉒営業ノルマ
⑬商品
⑫上座
⑱契約
⑲取引
⑭見積
⑮価格
⑯納期
⑰取引条件

of honor   ⑬product   ⑭estimate   ⑮price   ⑯delivery date   ⑰business terms   ⑱contract   ⑲deal   ⑳sales record   ㉑numerical sales target   ㉒sales quota   ㉓sales performance

chapter ❸ Salesperson

1 飛び込み営業する
I do some walk-in sales.

2 名刺交換する
I exchange business cards with someone.

3 取引先に直行直帰する
I visit a client and go home right after.

4 部下の外回りに同行する
I accompany my staff making the rounds to sell the product.

5 サンプルを持参する
I bring some samples with me.

tips
❶ walk-in は名詞で「[予約しない]飛び入りの客」の意味もある。e.g. No walk-ins.(一見さんお断り)
❸「直行直帰」に該当する語句はないので、このように表現する。
❹「得意先を回る」は make the rounds of my customers.
❺「[販促用]無料サンプル」は giveaway または freebie と言う。

6　ミスのおわびに伺い、平謝りする
I call on a client and make a full-scale apology for my mistake.

7　年始のあいさつに行く
I make New Year's calls.

8　身だしなみを整える
I check my appearance.

9　口臭に気をつける
I check my breath.

10　営業スマイルをキープする
I keep a [business] smile on my face.

❻ full-scale は「全面的な」。「誠意のある謝罪」は sincere apology。
❼ call は「[短い]訪問」のこと。
❽ 「身なりを整える」「正装する」は I spruce myself up. と言う。
❾ keep one's mouth odor-free で「口臭がしないようにする」。

chapter ❸ Salesperson

11 新規客を開拓する
I seek new customers.

12 営業電話をかける
I make a sales call.

13 商品を売り込む
I make a sales pitch.

14 新規サービスを紹介する
I explain a new service.

15 クライアントを研究する
I do research on my client.

tips

⓫ cultivate new customers でもよい。
⓬ 「[迷惑な]勧誘電話」は cold/blind call と言う。call は「訪問」でもあり、make a sales call には「営業訪問する」の意味もある。
⓭ pitch ~ to ... で「~を…に売り込む」。e.g. We'll pitch the product to pregnant mothers.（妊婦にその商品を売り込みます）

CD 1 **10**

16 見積を出す
I make an estimate.

17 価格の交渉をする
I negotiate a price.

18 取引条件を決める
I set the business terms.

19 営業トークで駆け引きする
I negotiate with a client while giving a sales talk.

20 代替案を出す
I offer <u>an alternative proposal</u> / <u>a backup plan</u>.

❶⓯「顧客のニーズを把握する」は understand the client's needs。
❶⓰「見積」は quotation、または quote とも言う。
❶⓱「価格を掛け合う」は haggle over the price。e.g. I haggle over the price with the shop owner.（店主と価格を掛け合う）
❶⓲ term は「条件」。e.g. payment terms（支払条件）、loan terms（融資条件）

chapter ❸ Salesperson

21 納期を再確認する
I double-check the delivery date.

22 上司に確認する
I check with my boss.

23 契約を結ぶ
I sign a contract.

24 売れ行きを調べる
I check the sales record.

tips

㉑ double-check は「二重のチェックをする、念を押す」の意味。confirm（確認する）と言ってもよい。
㉒ check with ~ は「~に聞いて確認する」。「~に照らし合わせて確認する」は check against ~。e.g. I check the report against the data.（データに照らし合わせて報告書を確認する）

25 取引先を接待する
I entertain a client.

26 目標数値を変更する
I revise the numerical sales target.

27 結果を出す
I achieve a result.

㉕「接待費」は entertainment expenses、「接待ゴルフ」は customer golf と言う。
㉖「目標数値を設定する」は set a numerical target。e.g. We set numerical targets for the reduction of office trash.（社内ゴミの量を削減する目標数値を設定しました）

chapter ❸ Salesperson

1. 先方はガードが固いから、アポを取るにも一苦労だ。
That client always has a guarded attitude so it's really tough just to make an appointment.

2. あちらの予定は空いてるかな。
I wonder if the client is available now.

3. ゲゲッ！ これって思い切りダブルブッキングじゃん。
No way! We ended up double-booking!

4. 先方にドタキャンされちゃったよ。
I got canceled on by a client at the last minute.

5. 名刺が切れそうだ。補充しなきゃ。
I'm running short of my business cards. I've got to top them up.

6. あそこの会社の担当者は、とにかく細かいから、気をつけて。
The person in charge there is meticulous about everything, so mind your P's and Q's.

guarded = 用心深い、慎重な／attitude = 態度／tough = 大変な／make an appointment = アポを取る

take a guarded stance to ~ で「~に慎重な態度を取る」。e.g. I feel they always take a guarded stance to us.（先方は当社に対して常にガードが固いように感じる）

I wonder if ~ = ~だろうか

available は「[人が] 時間がある」という意味。e.g. Please have a look at it when you're available.（お手すきの時にでもご覧下さい）。「[日時が] 都合のよい」は convenient。e.g Is Tuesday at 2 p.m. convenient for you?（火曜午後2時はご都合よろしいでしょうか）

No way! = あり得ない！／end up ~ = 結果として~になる

「あり得ない！」の意味では This can't be happening!（こんなこと実際に起きているはずがない）もよく使われる。e.g. All the data's gone? This can't be happening!（データが全部消えた？あり得ない！）

---

get canceled on = キャンセルされる／at the last minute = 土壇場で

「土壇場で取りやめる」は back out at the last minute とも。e.g. Mr. Doncam said he'd come to the year-end party but backed out at the last minute.（ドンカムさんは忘年会に来ると言ってたけどドタキャンしたよ）

---

be runing short of ~ = ~がなくなりかけている／top ~ up = ~を補充する

be short of ~ で「~が不足している、~を切らしている」の意味。e.g. I'm sorry. I'm short of business cards now.（すみません。いま名刺を切らしておりまして）

---

meticulous = 几帳面な／mind one's P's and Q's = 言動に注意する

mind one's P's and Q's は「p と q は似ている文字なので注意する」が元来の意味。ほかにアルファベットを使った面白い表現として dot the i's and cross the t's（i には点を t には横棒を忘れるな）がある。「細心の注意を払う」という意味。

chapter ❸ Salesperson

7 夏の外回りは汗だくになるなあ。
Making sales rounds in the summer makes me sweat.

---

8 まずは、クライアントに顔を印象づけないと。
I'm going to make a strong first impression on my client.

---

9 とにかく第一印象が肝心だよね。
A good first impression is everything, you know.

---

10 留守か。名刺だけ置いていこう。
He's not in now? Then I'll just leave my card.

---

11 まずは自分が商品を好きにならないとだめだな。
I guess I should love the product myself first.

---

12 営業は自分の話ばかりするんじゃなくて、相手の希望を聞き出さなきゃ。
As a salesperson, you shouldn't talk only about yourself but ask your client what he wants.

sales round = 外回りの営業／sweat = 汗をかく

反対に「内勤、デスクワーク」は desk/office work で OK。e.g. I did nothing but desk work today.（今日はデスクワークばかりだった）。「今日はうだるような暑さだ」は It's sweltering hot today.。

---

make an impression on ~ = ~に印象づける

「顔を覚えている」なら remember one's face、または know ~ by sight と言う。e.g. I know him by sight but don't remember his name.（顔は覚えているけど、名前が思い出せない）

---

everything = すべて／~, you know = ~でしょう

「肝心なことは、重要なのは~」は What counts most is ~ という表現もある。e.g. What counts most is leading a healthy life.（重要なのは健康な生活を送ることだよ）

---

be not in = 出社していない、社内にいない (= be out)／leave = ~を置いておく

留守していた人が名刺を見て後から電話をかけてきた場合、「担当者は今、席を外しています。伝言を承りましょうか」と言うときは、The person in charge is not in now. Would you like to leave a message?。

I guess ~ = ~と思う／first = まずは

「~を好きになる」は take to ~ でもよい。e.g. I took to our products when they were introduced on TV.（テレビで紹介されて自社製品が好きになった）

---

salesperson (= sales representative) = 営業マン

「人の話を聞く技術」は good listening skills。e.g. Learning good listening skills is vital for sales representatives.（人の話を上手に聞くスキルを身に付けることは、営業担当者にとって不可欠です）

chapter ❸ Salesperson

13 ちょっとした世間話ができるように、常にアンテナを張っておかなきゃ！
Since I need to small-talk with clients, I should always keep myself open to new ideas.

---

14 ルート営業ばっかりだとやりがいないな。
Just making regular sales visits to my regular clients is not rewarding.

---

15 新しい担当者にもしっかり売り込まなきゃ。
I better not forget to do a good demonstration of our products to the new person in charge.

---

16 あれ、この場合、上座はあそこになるのかな。
Hmm ... should the spot over there be the seat of honor for this table?

---

17 出されたお茶を飲むタイミングってけっこう悩むときあるよね。
Sometimes I really wonder when to start drinking the tea served to me.

---

18 お、なかなか好感触。これはイケるかも。
Looks like they like it a lot. Maybe I can go ahead with the sale.

small-talk with ~ = ~と世間話をする／keep oneself open to ~ = ~に対して心を開いておく、アンテナを張っておく

「好奇心旺盛である」なら have a great deal of curiosity。e.g. Ms. Nozey has a great deal of curiosity about everything happening in the office. (ノージーさんは社内で起きること全てに関して好奇心旺盛です)

---

regular sales visit to ~ = ~への定期的な営業訪問、ルート営業／regular client = 得意先／rewarding = やりがいのある

「ルート営業」は route（ルート）の派生語 routine（お決まりの）を使って、routine sales visits でもよい。e.g. I'm bored with my routine sales visits. (お決まりの営業訪問にあきてしまった)

---

better not ~ = ~しない方がよい／do a demonstration = [商品]説明をする、宣伝する／person in charge = 担当者

「しつこく売り込む、うるさく勧める」は tout と言う。e.g. You don't have to tout your product. It sells itself. (その商品をしつこく宣伝する必要はないよ。自然に売れるものだから)

---

spot = 場所／the seat of honor = 上座

「テーブルの上座に座る」は take the head of the table。e.g. I wonder who's going to take the head of the table tonight. (今夜は誰が上座に着くことになるのだろう)

---

when to ~ = いつ~すべきか／served to ~ = ~に出された

serve ~ to ... で「…に~（食べ物・飲み物）を出す」の意味。e.g. I serve tea to a client. (客にお茶を出します)、All I ever do at the office is serve tea to my boss. (オフィスでの私の仕事は上司のお茶くみばかり)

---

look like ~ = ~のようだ／go ahead with ~ = ~を進める

「~から好感触を得る」は receive a positive response from~。e.g. Our online service has been receiving positive responses from shoppers. (当社のオンラインサービスはお客様よりよい評価を頂戴しております)。

chapter 3 Salesperson

19 いったん社に持ち帰って検討します。
I'll think over this offer in the office later.

---

20 さっきの担当者の女性、感じ悪かったなあ。クライアントだからって、あんなに威張らなくても。
The lady in charge was so mean! How can clients be so stuck-up?

---

21 海山商事のスペイダーさんは、手ごわい相手だから気合を入れないと。
Mr. Spader from Umiyama trading company is a tough negotiator, so I'm going to give it all I've got.

---

22 昔からのお客さんとの話は気心が知れてるからラクだ。
It's easy talking with old clients because I know them inside out.

---

23 なじみだからと言って、すぐに仕事を回してくれるご時世じゃなくなったなあ。
People won't offer you a job that easily these days, no matter how close you are to them.

---

24 この商品、どのクライアントも食いつきいいみたい。
As I see it, every client takes a strong interest in this merchandise.

think over ~ = ~をじっくり検討する

逆に「その場で下す決断」を on-the-spot decision と言う。e.g. I'm afraid we can't make an on-the-spot decision here.（すみませんが、この場では決断することは出来かねます）

---

mean = 意地悪な／stuck-up = 生意気な、お高くとまった

How can/could ~? は「どうして～できるのか[、できるわけがない]」という反語を意味する疑問文。e.g. How could you say that to your colleague?（どうして同僚にそんなことが言えるの）

---

trading company = 商社／tough negotiator = 手ごわい交渉人

give it all one's got で「持っているものを出し切って全力を尽くす、努力する」の意味。give it one's all も同じ意味の表現。e.g. Give it your all!（全力で頑張れ！）

---

know ~ inside out = ~について裏も表も知っている

悪い意味での「馴れ合いの関係」は cozy relationship と言う。e.g. I know the company maintains a cozy relationship with the government but ...（会社がずっと政府と馴れ合いの関係にあるのは知っているんだけど…）

---

no matter how ~(= however ~) = どんなに～でも

「仕事上の知人」は business acquaintance と言う。e.g. In this cold world, business acquaintances won't be of much help in finding a job.（この世知辛い世の中では、仕事上の知人は職探しにはあまり役に立ってくれないなあ）

---

as I see it = 見たところ／take an interest in ~ = ~に興味を持つ／merchandise = 商品

go for ~ にも「～が気に入る、～に食いつく」の意味がある。e.g. Most children go for Disney movies.（ほとんどの子どもはディズニー映画に飛びつく）

chapter ❸ Salesperson

25 やっぱり回転の速い商品しか置いてくれないなあ。
I knew they'd only allow fast-selling items on the shelf.

---

26 悔しい〜！ ライバル社の商品の方が目立ってる。
Argh, how frustrating! Obviously, our rival's product is more eye-catching than ours.

---

27 不景気のせいか、お客さんの財布のひもが固くなったなあ。
I think it's probably because of the economic downturn, but customers these days keep a tight hold on their purse strings.

---

28 強引な売り込みは嫌われるだけだよ。
You'll only get rejected if you press someone to buy your stuff.

---

29 売りっぱなしじゃなくて、アフターフォローも大事にしないと。
You can't just sell the products; you should give the same importance to good follow-through service.

---

30 あんな大口のクライアントを引き継ぐなんて、私には荷が重すぎる。
Taking over such a big client is too big a burden for me.

I knew ~ = ~と思ってた、やっぱり~だ／fast-selling = すぐに売れる、回転のよい

「[商品・在庫・客などの] 回転」は turnover と言う。e.g. This coffee shop has good customer turnover. (この喫茶店は客の回転がよい)

Argh = もう! ああ~／rival's product = 競合商品／eye-catching = 目立つ

「人目を引く商品、目玉商品」は eye-catcher と言う。e.g. I believe this is going to be the eye-catcher for today's event. (これは今日のイベントの目玉になるに違いない)

---

economic downturn(= recession) = 景気の悪化、不況／keep a tight hold on one's purse strings = 財布のひもをしっかり締めておく

「財布のひもをゆるめる」は loosen one's purse strings、「財布のひもを握る」は control the purse strings と言う。e.g. My wife controls the purse strings. (妻が財布のひもを握ってるんだ)

---

get rejected = 拒絶される、嫌われる／press ~ to ... = ~に…するように催促する、うるさくせがむ

「押し売り、強引な販売」を hard sell (反対は soft sell) と言う。e.g. Giving them the hard sell is never the best tactic. (強引に売り込むことは決して最上の策ではない)

---

give importance to ~ = ~を重要視する／follow-through service = アフターサービス

アフターフォローはアフターサービス同様カタカナ英語。正しくは follow-through/after-sale service と言うことに注意。

---

take over ~ = ~を引き継ぐ／burden = 重荷

take over は take over as ~ で「~の職を引き継ぐ」という意味でもよく使われる。e.g. As of April 1st, Mr. Uhlman will take over as accounting director. (4月1日付でウールマンさんが経理部長を引き継ぎます)

chapter ❸ Salesperson

31 今回はフォクセン社に持っていかれるかなあ。
I'm afraid this one will be carried off by Foxen Inc.

32 この案件がまとまると大きいんだけどな。
I think it's going to be a really big deal if I get it all sewn up.

33 だいぶ頑張って見積書出したんだから、うまくいくといいけど。
I buckled down and finished up the estimate. I hope it's all right.

34 もっと金額を抑えて、何としてでもこの受注を取らなきゃ。
Whatever it takes, I must get them to place the order with me by offering a lower price.

35 大口契約取った！　最高の気分だ！
I got a big sales contract, and I'm feeling on top of the world!

36 やった！　上半期売り上げナンバーワンになったぞ！
Yes! Now I'm the top salesperson for the first half of the year!

carry ~ off = 〜をさらっていく、奪っていく

「〜をさっと奪い去る」は swoop away ~。e.g. The manager came in and swooped away the document from under my nose.（部長が入ってきて、僕の目の前でその書類をさっと奪っていったよ）

---

deal = 取引／get ~ sewn up = 〜を取りまとめる（sewnはsewの過去分詞形）

sew up ~ は「〜を上手くまとめる」。e.g. It's sewn up.（＜契約や取り決めが＞これで確定だ）。なお、deal を使った It's a deal.（これで商談成立だ）もよく使われる表現。

---

buckle down = 専念する／finish up ~ = 〜を仕上げる／estimate = 見積

buckle は「留め金、バックル」のこと。buckle down（留め金で下に固定される）から「その場にがっちり居座る、身を入れる」の意味になる。なお、buckle up には「シートベルトを締める」の意味がある。

---

whatever it takes = 何としても／get ~ to ... = 〜に…させる／place an order with ~ = 〜に注文を出す

「何としてでも」は whatever happens でもよい。e.g. Whatever happens, I'm going to get their agreement.（何としてもイエスと言わせてみせるぞ）

---

contract = 契約／feel on top of the world = 最高の気分である

「最高の気分」を意味する表現は多くあるが、be on cloud nine（至福の状態だ）、be in seventh heaven（幸福の絶頂だ）はともに宗教に由来し、数字を使った表現として興味深い。

Yes! = よし!、やった!／salesperson = 販売員、営業担当者／the first half of the year = 上半期

「営業成績」は sales performance と言う。e.g. I got a No. 1 ranking in annual sales performance.（年間販売業績ランキングで1位になった）

chapter ❸ Salesperson

37 今回は商談がまとまらなかったけど、次につなげることができた。
I couldn't pull it off this time, but at least the negotiation gave me a clue for the next round.

---

38 彼女は、人の懐に飛び込むのがうまいから営業向きだね。
I think she's got what it takes to be a salesperson because she pretty much gets along with everybody.

---

39 土日どっちも接待ゴルフ。身が持たない。
I'm taking clients golfing both on Saturday and Sunday ... I can't take it anymore.

---

40 最近経費削られてきついよ。
Recently, management has cut expenses, and I have to work on a strict budget now.

---

41 今期は、ノルマがきついなあ。達成できるかな。
The sales quota this quarter is set so high I wonder if I can meet it.

---

42 売れない物を売るのが営業だよ。
You know, a salesperson is someone who sells things that don't sell themselves.

pull ~ off = ~を上手くやってのける／at least = 少なくとも／clue for ~ = ~への手がかり

「商談をまとめる」は正式には clinch a deal、または conclude a bargain と言う。e.g. We concluded a bargain with Ternip Inc. last week. （当社は先週、ターニップ社との契約を成立させた）

---

what it takes to ~ = ~するのに必要な性質／get along with ~ = ~と仲良く付き合う

「懐に飛び込む」は「歩調を合わせる」なので get along with ~ で表現。「誰からも好かれる」は be all things to all people。e.g. I can't be all things to all people. （誰からも好かれる人にはなれないなあ）

---

take ~ golfing = ~をゴルフに連れて行く／can't take it = 耐えられない

「これ以上無理、限界だ」を意味する表現としては、I can't <u>bear/stand</u> it. （もう我慢できない）、I've had it. （もう十分だ）、I'm at my breaking point. （身体的に限界だ）、This is the last straw. （もう辛抱ならない）などがある。

---

management = 経営陣／cut expenses = 予算・経費を削減する／on a strict budget = 厳しい予算で

「経費を極度に切り詰める」ならば to the bone （骨の髄まで、徹底的に）を使って、cut expenses to the bone と言う。

---

sales quota = 売上・販売ノルマ／quarter = 四半期／I wonder if ~ = ~かどうか疑問だ／meet ~ = ~を満たす、達成する

quota は「割り当て量、ノルマ」の意味。e.g. Though it was tough, I managed to fulfill my quota. （きつかったけど、何とかノルマを達成できた）

---

sell oneself = [放っておいても]自然に売れる

「売れない商品」は unsellable goods または unmarketable products とも言う。e.g. They say there are several ways to turn unsellable goods into salable ones. （売れない商品を売れる商品へと変える方法がいくつかあると言うんだけど）。

Skit 営業編

売り上げナンバーワンが「営業のコツ」を伝授

Woman: You know, I'm new to the sales department[1]. I have to meet clients and tell them about our new goods, but I'm nervous[2].

Man: Well, I was the top salesperson for the first half of the year. I got a big sales contract and I'm feeling on top of the world. I think I can help you.

W: I know I should always check my appearance and my breath. What else?

M: A good first impression is everything, you know. You should try to make a strong impression on your clients. And you shouldn't talk only about yourself, but ask your clients what they want.

W: That's good advice.

M: You know, a salesperson is someone who sells things that don't sell themselves. Here's[3] another trick[4] I learned. The catalog is not enough. I always bring some samples with me to give to the client[5]. They like that.

W: Thank you so much! I feel much more confident[6] now.

女性：ほら、私、営業部門って初めてでしょ。新商品の売り込みのためにクライアントに会わなくちゃいけないんだけど、緊張しちゃって。
男性：いやあ、僕は上半期の売り上げトップでさ。大口の契約を取り付けて最高の気分なんだ。力になれると思うけど。
女：身だしなみと口臭には常に気を付けるべし、というのは心得てるわ。ほかに何かある？
男：とにかく第一印象が肝心だよ。まずは顔を覚えてもらわなきゃ。それに自分の話ばかりするんじゃなくて、相手の希望を聞き出すこと。
女：いいアドバイスだわ。
男：いいかい、売れないものを売るのが営業だからね。もう一つ僕が学んだコツがある。カタログだけじゃ不十分なんだ。僕はいつもクライアントへの置き土産用に商品サンプルを持ち歩いているんだけど、これは評判いいよ。
女：ありがとう！ おかげでだいぶ自信がついてきたわ。

【語注】

❶ sales department: 営業部
❷ nervous: 神経質な、緊張した
❸ Here's ~.: ~がありますよ。
❹ trick: コツ、やり方、策略
❺ client: 顧客
❻ confident: 自信に満ちた、確信して

Quick Check

本章に出てきたフレーズを復習しましょう。以下の日本語の意味になるよう
英文を完成させてください。答えはページの下にあります。

❶飛び込み営業する。 ➡P076
I do some (　　　) (　　　).

❷年始のあいさつに行く。 ➡P077
I (　　　) New Year's (　　　).

❸商品を売り込む。 ➡P078
I (　　　) a sales (　　　).

❹ゲゲッ! これって思い切りダブルブッキングじゃん。 ➡P082
(　　　) (　　　)! We (　　　) (　　　) double-booking!

❺名刺が切れそうだ。補充しなきゃ。 ➡P082
I'm (　　　) (　　　) (　　　) my (　　　) (　　　). I've got to (　　　) them (　　　).

❻ちょっとした世間話ができるように、常にアンテナを張っておかなきゃ! ➡P086
Since I need to (　　　) with clients, I should always (　　　) (　　　) (　　　) to (　　　) (　　　).

❼いったん社に持ち帰って検討します。 ➡P088
I'll (　　　) (　　　) this offer in the office (　　　).

❽昔からのお客さんとの話は気心が知れてるからラクだ。 ➡P088
It's (　　　) (　　　) with (　　　) clients because I know (　　　) (　　　) (　　　).

❾悔しい〜! ライバル社の商品の方が目立ってる。 ➡P090
Argh, how (　　　)! Obviously, our (　　　) product is more (　　　) than ours.

❿最近経費削られてきついよ。 ➡P094
Recently, management has (　　　) (　　　), and I have to work (　　　) (　　　) (　　　) (　　　) (　　　) now.

❶walk-in/sales ❷make/calls ❸make/pitch ❹No/way/ended/up ❺running/short/of/business/cards/top/up ❻small-talk/keep/myself/open/new/ideas ❼think/over/later ❽easy/talking/old/them/inside/out ❾frustrating/rival's/eye-catching ❿cut/expenses/on/a/strict/budget

chapter 4

出張
Business Trips

会社員には出張する機会も多いもの。
準備や下調べをして初めての土地に
乗り込み、何らかの成果を上げる。
状況が許せば、ついでに観光も。
いつもとは違った場所にいると、
いろいろなことに思いを馳せます。

chapter 4 Business Trips

Words 単語編

❶荷造り ❷宿泊 ❸航空券
❹飛行機の便 ❺新幹線
❻指定席 ❼自由席
❽期間限定弁当

❿コインロッカー

❾荷物

⓫ビジネスホテル
⓬モーニングコール

❶packing ❷accommodation ❸air ticket ❹flight ❺bullet train ❻reserved seat ❼unreserved seat ❽seasonal lunch box ❾baggage ❿[coin] locker ⓫business hotel ⓬wake-up call

まずは、さまざまな物や事の名前で
「出張」のシーンのイメージをつかもう。

⓮工場見学
⓯会社案内
⓰本社
⓱支社
⓲見本
⓳人脈

⓭スケジュール表

⓴郷土料理

㉓出張費
㉔時差ぼけ

㉑土地の名物
㉒お土産

⓭schedule ⓮plant tour ⓯corporate brochure ⓰head office ⓱branch office ⓲sample ⓳network of connections ⓴local cuisine ㉑local specialties ㉒gift ㉓travel expenses ㉔jet lag

chapter 4 Business Trips

1 出張申請する
I ask to go on a business trip.

2 宿泊と交通の手配をする
I make arrangements for travel and accommodation.

3 総務に上海出張の航空券と宿泊の手配依頼を出す
I ask the general affairs department to arrange the air tickets and accommodation for my business trip to Shanghai.

4 2泊3日の出張の準備をする
I prepare for a three-day, two-night business trip.

5 出張中の行動予定表を作成する
I make a schedule for my business trip.

tips

❷ accommodation は「宿泊[施設]」、make travel arrangements で「旅行の手配をする」。
❹「2泊3日の出張」は a business trip of three days and two nights とも言う。「1週間の出張」なら one-week business trip。
❺「予定表」は timetable と言ってもよい。

6 留守中の担当者を指名する
I choose someone to be in charge while I'm away.

7 海外出張中に使う携帯をレンタルする
I rent a cellphone to use during my overseas business trip.

8 支店に顔を出す
I drop by the branch office.

9 工場見学をする
I go on a plant tour.

10 店舗調査する
I conduct a store audit.

❻ be in charge は「担当して」、while I'm away は「私がいない間」。
❽ drop by (立ち寄る) のかわりに visit (訪れる) でもよい。
❾ plant は「工場」。I take a factory tour. でも同じ意味。
❿ audit は「監査、[会計] 検査」。「現地調査をする」なら conduct an on-site investigation。

chapter ❹ Business Trips

11 支店開設準備をする
I prepare to open a new branch [office].

12 最新システムの視察に行く
I go to inspect the latest system[s].

13 取引先の人と初対面のあいさつを交わす
I exchange greetings with the client.

14 悪天候で足止めを食う
I am held up by the bad weather [on my business trip].

tips

⓫ branch office は「支店、支社」。⓯の head office は「本店、本社」。
⓬ inspect は「視察する、調べる」、「最新の」は newest でも同じ。
⓭「あいさつする」は greet。「商談をする」は discuss a business matter。
⓯「私に連絡してください」なら Please keep me posted.。
⓰「出張から急いで日帰りする」は I come back from my business trip

15 本社に連絡を入れる
I contact my head office.

16 出張先からとんぼ返りをする
I rush back from my business trip.

17 部署にお土産を買って帰る
I buy gifts for people in my section.

18 出張費を立て替える
I pay for my business travel expenses [which will be reimbursed later].

quickly without staying overnight. と言う。
⓱「部署の同僚に」は for my co-workers in my department としてもよい。「お土産」は souvenir だと「記念品」の意味合いが強くなるので、ここでは gift が適切。
⓲ be reimbursed は「払い戻してもらう」。

chapter 4 Business Trips

1. 英語圏以外の海外出張は初めてだから緊張するなぁ。
It's my first [overseas] business trip to a non-English-speaking country, so I'm rather nervous.

2. 予算内だと、このホテルしかないかなあ。
This is probably the only hotel within our [set] budget.

3. ヨーロッパまでエコノミークラスとは、うちもコスト管理が厳しくなったなあ。
We have to travel economy-class to Europe. Our company's budget control is very tight now.

4. 不況のあおりで、出張回数が減ったなあ。
We don't have as many business trips as we used to because of the economic downturn.

5. 滞在時間が2時間、移動時間が8時間の日帰り出張か。疲れるだろうなあ。
It's a one-day business trip with eight hours of traveling for a two-hour visit... I'll be totally worn out.

6. 効率良く回れるようにスケジュール組まなきゃ。
I need to work out my schedule so that I can go around places without wasting time.

It's my first ~ = 私の初めての〜だ／**overseas** = 海外の／**non-English-speaking country** = 英語圏ではない国 cf. English-speaking countries = 英語圏[の国々]／**rather** = かなり

「緊張する」でなく「ワクワクする」なら I'm quite excited。

---

probably = おそらく、たぶん／**the only~** = 唯一の／**within budget** = 予算内で

set budget は「決められた（設定された）予算」。「予算をオーバーする、超える」は go over／exceed the budget。

---

economy-class(= coach [class]) = エコノミークラス[で] cf. first class = ファーストクラス | business class = ビジネスクラス／**travel to ~** = 〜まで旅行する／**budget control** = 予算管理／**tight** = きつい

「搭乗券をビジネスクラスにアップグレードした」は I upgraded my ticket from economy class to business class. と言う。

---

as many ~ as … = …と同じだけの数の〜／**used to ~** = 以前は〜だった（後ろに have business trips が省略されている）／**economic downturn** = 不況
cf. downturn = 下降、低迷

前半を直訳すると「以前と同じぐらいの回数の出張はない」となる。「不況」はほかに sluggish economy、recession などとも言える。

---

one-day = 一日の／**traveling** = 移動／**totally** = 完全に、すっかり／**worn out** = くたびれはてる（worn は wear の過去分詞形）cf. I'm worn out. = くたくただ

「日帰り旅行」は a day／one-day trip、「一泊旅行」なら overnight trip になる。

---

work out ~ = 〜を考え出す、[計画・予定]を立てる／**go around ~** = 〜を歩き回る、あちこちに行く／**without ~** = 〜することなしに／**waste time** = 時間を無駄にする

「一つの場所から次へと移動する」は move from one place to another。

chapter 4 Business Trips

7 ネットの経路探索ってすごく便利。
Finding the [most direct] route [to the destination] on the Internet is really convenient!

8 スケジュール表は出張者名簿と一緒に、事前に先方に送っておこう。
I'll send them our schedule with the list of the employees who will go there.

9 名刺(会社案内／サンプル)は多めに持って行かなきゃ。
I have to [remember to] bring enough business cards (corporate brochures / samples).

10 パソコンに必要なデータを全て落として、持っていこう。
I'll put all the data I need on my PC and bring it with me.

11 電車内でもネットが利用できるなんて、便利になったなあ。
We can even use the Internet on the train now. How convenient!

12 行きの新幹線の中で、書類に目を通そう。
I'll look through the document on the Shinkansen on the way there.

find ~ on the Internet = ~をインターネットで見つける cf. find ~ on the Netでもよい／**the most direct route** = 最短距離、最短ルート cf. route = 経路、道筋／**destination** = 目的地、行き先

「インターネットで検索する」は search the Internet/Net と言う。

---

send ~ with ... = …と共に~を送る／**list** = 一覧表／**employees who will go there** = そこに行く予定の社員

「事前に」を強調したければ beforehand や in advance を our schedule の後に入れてもよい。

---

enough = 十分な／**business card** = 名刺／**corporate** = 会社の、企業の／**brochure** = パンフレット、小冊子

「名刺を交換する」は exchange business cards。「名刺をいただけますでしょうか」は May I have your business card? と言う。

---

put ~ on a PC = ~をパソコンに入れる／**bring ~ with me** = ~を持って行く、持参する

ノートパソコンは laptop [computer]、または notebook [computer]。「パソコンにソフトを入れる（インストールする）」場合は install software on my PC となる。

---

even = ~でさえも／**use the Internet** = インターネットを使う／**How ~ !** = なんて~なんだ!(感嘆、驚きを表す表現)／**convenient** = 便利な

「インターネットに接続する」は access / connect to the Internet、「インターネット接続料金」は Internet access fee。

---

look through ~ = ~に目を通す、調べる cf. go throughでもよい／**document** = 書類／**on the way** = ~の途中で

「帰って来る途中で」は on the way back [here]。新幹線はそのままでも使えるが、英語で言うなら bullet train（弾丸列車）。

chapter 4 Business Trips

13 期間限定(春限定)の駅弁を試すのが楽しみ。
I'm looking forward to trying the <u>seasonal bento (special lunch box for spring only)</u>.

14 部長とずっと一緒だから、気が張るなあ。まさか、部長と相部屋じゃないよね。
I'm nervous because I'll be with my boss the whole time. I won't be sharing a room with him, will I?

15 モーニングコール(ランドリーサービス)を頼んでおこう。
I'll have to ask for a <u>wake-up call (laundry service)</u>.

16 ボードを持った出迎えの人が来てくれてるはずなんだけど、ちゃんと会えるといいなあ。
There is supposed to be someone with a sign to pick me up here. I hope I can find that person all right.

17 この人が木下さんか。メールよりも感じのよさそうな人でよかった。
So, this is Mr. Kinoshita. He seems much nicer in person than through e-mail.

18 電話やメールだけのやりとりと違って、顔を知ってるといろいろやりやすくなるね。
When you've spoken to someone face-to-face instead of just contacting via phone and e-mail, you can work with them much more easily.

look forward to ~ = ～するのを楽しみに待つ(toの後の動詞はing形)／**try** = 試す／**seasonal** = 季節の cf. season = 季節／**lunch box** = 弁当／**for ~ only** = ～限定

「駅弁」を英語で説明するなら a boxed <u>meal</u>/<u>lunch</u> sold at stations and on trains となる。

---

the whole time = ずっと、全ての時間／**share a room** = 相部屋になる、[人と]同室になる／**I won't be~, will I?** = ～するようなことはないでしょうね?(付加疑問文、**won't** = will not)

「ホテルに泊まる」は stay at a hotel、「一人部屋」は single room。

---

ask for ~ = ～を頼む／**a wake-up call** = モーニングコール cf. (×)morning callは和製英語なので注意／**laundry** = 洗濯 cf. dry cleaning = ドライクリーニング

「[7時に]モーニングコールをお願いします」は I'd like a wake-up call [at 7:00], please. と言う。

---

supposed to be ~ = ～することになっている、するはずだ／**sign** = 表示、標識 cf. signboard = 掲示板／**pick ~ up** = ～を迎えに来る／**I hope ~** = ～と願っている／**all right** = ちゃんと、確かに

There is someone ~ だと「誰かが来ている」と断定する言い方。

He seems nice = いい人のようだ／**much** = とても／**in person** = じかに、直接に／**through ~** = ～を通して

「直接会う」は meet in person。「～に対する第一印象」は my first impression of ~。

---

face-to-face = 直接、顔を合わせて、cf. face-to-face talk = 直接交渉、膝詰め談判／**instead of ~** = ～の代わりに／**contact** = 連絡をとる／**via ~** = ～によって／**much more easily** = もっと簡単に

「電話かメールで連絡ください」なら Please contact <u>me</u>/<u>us</u> by phone or e-mail.。

chapter 4 Business Trips

19 キーパーソンに会えたのは大きな収穫だ。
It was useful to meet the key person.

20 先方の事情で出張が急きょキャンセルになった。
My business trip was suddenly canceled because of a problem on the other side.

21 海外出張中の部長に今すぐ連絡つくかな?
Can we get in contact with the manager who is on an overseas business trip right now?

22 出張費使ってはるばる来たんだから、何か成果を残さなくちゃ。
I have to produce some results, since I came all the way here using company travel expenses.

23 何とか商談がまとまった。わざわざ来たかいがあったな。
We managed to close a deal. It was worth coming all the way here.

24 資料を見るだけなのと、現地に足を運んで実際に見るのとではずいぶん違うなあ。
Coming to and seeing the actual place with your own eyes is really different from just looking at the documents.

useful = 有益な、好都合だ／**key person** = かぎとなる人物、キーパーソン

key person は「かぎとなる人物」で、「責任者」「担当者」とは限らない。「責任者」「担当者」なら the person in charge と言う。

---

cancel = 中止する、取り消す（受身 **be canceled** で「取り消された、キャンセルになった」）／**the other side** = 相手側

「出張がぎりぎりになって［間際に］キャンセルになった」なら My business trip was canceled at the last minute.。

---

get in contact with ~ = ~と連絡を取る／**on a trip** = 旅行中で／**right now** = 今すぐに

「部長」manager の代わりに「上司」boss でも可。「連絡がありましたか？」なら Did you hear [anything] from him/her? 「連絡が取れない」は I can't reach / get a hold of him/her.。

---

produce = 作り出す、生み出す／**result** = 結果 cf. produce a result で「結果を生む、成果を出す」／**all the way** = ［遠いところへ］わざわざ／**travel expenses** = 旅費

「成果なく終わった」なら I couldn't produce any results. や We came up empty-handed.（empty-handed = 手に何も持たずに、何の収穫もなく）。

---

manage to ~ = 何とか~する／**close a deal** = 取引・商談をまとめる、成立させる cf. deal = 取引、契約／**worth ~ing** = ~する価値がある

「わざわざ来たかいがあった」は The long trip was well worth it. と言ってもよい。

---

actual = 実際の／**see ~ with one's own eyes** = 自分自身の目で~を見る、目の当たりにする／**document** = 書類、資料

「今何が起こっているか調べる」なら check what's going on。ことわざの「百聞は一見にしかず」は Seeing is believing.（見ることは信じることだ）。

chapter 4 Business Trips

25 今回の一番の収穫は、普段見られない、地方の売り場に行けたこと。
The best part of my trip was being able to go to the local shops that I don't usually have the chance to see.

---

26 とりあえず、今回は人脈が作れただけでもよしとしよう。
Anyway, I will have to settle for having built up a network of connections.

---

27 早く仕事片付けて、遊んじゃおっと。
I will get this work done quickly so that I can go out and have some fun!

---

28 予定がびっしりで、観光なんかできるわけないよ。
My schedule is too tight! I have no time for sightseeing.

---

29 どんな出張でも、土地の名物を食べるのが、醍醐味だよね。
Eating local specialties is the best part of any business trip.

---

30 領収書を一部なくしちゃったけど、出張費の精算できるかなあ。
I've lost some receipts, and I wonder if I can get my travel expenses paid back.

the best part of ~ = ~の一番いいところ／**local** = 地元の、その地域の／
have the chance to ~ = ~する機会がある

後半は直訳すると「普段は訪れる機会のない地域の店舗に行くことができた」となる。

---

anyway = とにかく、なにしろ／**settle for ~** = ~でよしとする、妥結する／**have built up** = 作り上げた（**built**は**build**の過去・過去分詞形）／**a network of connections** = 人脈 cf. connection = つながり、関係

networking は「仕事上のネットワーク（交流・人脈）作り」。

---

get ~ done = ~を終わらせる／**so that ~** = ~できるように／**go out** = 出かける／**have fun** = 楽しむ

「今日の仕事は終わった」は、We're done for today.、That does it for today.、「今日の仕事はもう終わりにしよう」は Let's call it a day! と言う。

---

tight = きつい、厳しい cf.スケジュールがきつい場合はhardではなくtightを使うのが普通／**have no time for ~** = ~のための時間がない／**sightseeing** = 観光 cf. do sightseeing = 観光する

後半は There's no way I can go sightseeing! と言ってもよい。

---

specialty = 名物、自慢料理／**the best part of ~** = ~の最高の部分、醍醐味／**any** = どんな~でも

「地元の食べ物を食べる」は eat local food、「ここの名産は何ですか？」と聞くなら What is the specialty here? と言えばよい。

I've lost = なくした（**lost**は**lose**の過去・過去分詞形）／**receipt** = レシート、領収書／**I wonder if ~** = ~かどうかと疑問に思う／**pay back** = 払い戻す cf. reimburse = 払い戻す、返金する

「領収書をください」は I would like a receipt, please.、「領収書は全部取っておかないと」は I have to keep all my receipts. と言う。

chapter 4 Business Trips

31 わざわざ出張することなかった気もするけど、おいしい物食べられたからよしとしよう。
I don't think I needed to come all the way here on a business trip, but I had some delicious food, so it was OK.

32 今度はプライベートの旅行で来たいなあ。
I'd like to come here just to travel for pleasure next time.

33 時差ぼけが抜けないなあ。
I can't get over this jet lag.

need to ~ = ~する必要がある／delicious food = おいしい食べ物

「これはおいしい！」は It's <u>delicious</u>/<u>tasty</u>!、It tastes good! などと言う。「おいしいごちそうを満喫した」は I really enjoyed the delicious food.。

I'd like to ~ = ~したいと思う(I'd = I would)

I'd like to come here just <u>for sightseeing</u>(<u>on vacation</u>) next time. 「次は観光で（休暇で）来たい」と言い換えてもよい。

---

get over ~ = 回復する、治る／jet lag = 時差ぼけ

「時差」は time difference。「時差ぼけだ」は I'm jet-lagged. または I have jet lag.、「時差ぼけでとても眠い（ぼーっとしている）」は I'm <u>very sleepy</u>(<u>absent-minded</u>) because of jet lag. と言う。

「起き寝る」流・ビジネス英語 その❷

基本的なビジネスメールの書き方

　インターネットが発達した現在、実際に相手と面と向かって英語で商談するよりも、ビジネスメールによって商品の発注や取引をする機会の方が多い。その場で言い直しができる会話とは違い、ビジネスメールではより慎重な内容が求められる。ここでは、英語でビジネスメールを書くためのヒントを紹介しよう。

1. ビジネスメールのマナー

友人に書くメールとは違い、ビジネスメールは相手が時間をかけて読んでくれるとは限らない。こちらの用件を的確に伝えるためには以下のポイントに気をつけよう。
・定型に沿って書く（下記の「ビジネスメールの構成」を参照）。
・簡潔でわかりやすい文で書くよう心掛ける。
・難解な語彙や抽象的な表現の使用を避ける。
・日付・時間・数値は具体的に記載する。

2. ビジネスメールの構成

以下のパターンに沿って文章を書くことで、こちらの用件をより確実に伝えることができる。

1. Subject line（件名）

相手の注意を引くためにも、簡潔に用件を要約した件名にする。
e.g. Inquiry about ...（…に関する問い合わせ）／ Request for ...（…の請求）
　　 Quotation for ...（…の見積もり）／ Confirmation of ...（…の確認）

2. Greeting（挨拶）

相手とメールの内容（フォーマル度）に合わせて、DearまたはHelloを用いる。
e.g. Dear Sir or Madam（拝啓、ご担当者の方）　＊個人名が不明な場合
　　 Hello, Mr. Johnson（こんにちは、ジョンソンさん）　＊より一般的な呼び掛け方

武藤克彦　Text by Katsuhiko Muto

3. Body（本文）

以下の段落構成を踏まえて、簡潔な文章で書く。

❶書き出し（メールを送った目的、または何に対する返信かを明確に述べる）

e.g. I'm writing to ...（…のためにご連絡差し上げます）

　　 This is in response to ...（これは…に対する返信です）

❷用件（提案、注文などは単刀直入に、辞退、謝罪などは気遣う表現や理由を書く）

e.g. Would you please send ...?（…を送っていただけませんでしょうか）

　　 I'm very sorry to inform you ...（残念ながら…をお伝えします）

❸結び（確認、謝罪、感謝、期待などの決まり文句で締めくくる）

e.g. We would appreciate it if you could ...（…していただければ幸いです）

　　 I look forward to -ing ...（…できることを楽しみにしております）

4. Closing line（締辞）

相手とフォーマル度に合わせて選択する。同じ相手なら毎回同じ表現を使う。

e.g. Sincerely yours、Yours sincerely ＊正式な文書に用いる非常に硬い表現

　　 Best regards、Best wishes ＊より一般的な表現

5. Signature（署名）

名前、役職、部署、会社名（連絡先）の順。あらかじめ作成・登録しておくとよい。

e.g. Kenta Nakajima（名前）

　　 Assistant Manager（役職名）

　　 Marketing Department（部署名）

　　 Japan Tele-Net Trading, Co.（会社名）

　こちらが英語ノンネイティブであることを相手が理解してくれると期待してはならない。ニュアンスや表現を完璧に伝えるのは難しいが、常に誤字や脱字には気をつけ、できるだけ正確な文章を書くように心掛けよう。

Skit 出張編

南米出張、準備は万端やる気はマンマン

Woman: **The boss asked me to go on a business trip to Venezuela[1].**
Man: **Wow, that's great!**
W: **Well, I have to make arrangements for travel and accommodation myself.**
M: **Oh, too bad.**
W: **No, finding the route on the Internet is really convenient.**
M: **Oh, that's good. What does he want you to do there?**
W: **I have to take a factory tour, conduct a store audit and prepare to open a new branch.**
M: **Oh, you'll have to take a lot of documents[2].**
W: **No, I'll put all the data I need on my PC and take it with me.**
M: **You'll enjoy it. It's a beautiful country.**
W: **But my schedule will be too tight. I won't have any time for sightseeing.**
M: **You'd better[3] buy some gifts for the people in this section.**
W: **Yes, the best part will be going to local shops you wouldn't be able to see anywhere else.**

女性：ボスが私に、ベネズエラに出張してくれって。
男性：ワオ、すごいじゃないか！
女：ええと、交通とか宿泊の手配をしなきゃ。
男：う～ん、そりゃ大変だね。
女：そうでもないのよ。ネットでの経路探索ってすっごく便利だから。
男：ああ、そりゃいいや。ボスはベネズエラで何をやれって？
女：工場見学に、店舗調査に、新しい支店の立ち上げの準備もしなきゃいけないの。
男：そうか、書類もたくさん持ってかなきゃいけないわけだ。
女：ううん、必要なデータはすべてパソコンに落として持ってくから。
男：楽しいだろうなあ。素晴らしい国だからねえ。
女：でも、予定がびっしりで観光なんかできるわけないわ。
男：この部署へのお土産は買って帰るんだよ。
女：ええ、出張の醍醐味はほかのどこにもないような地元のお店に行くことですもんね。

【語注】

❶ Venezuela: ベネズエラ（南米北部の共和国）
❷ document: 書類
❸ you'd better ~: ～した方がいい、～するべきだ

Quick Check

本章に出てきたフレーズを復習しましょう。以下の日本語の意味になるよう
英文を完成させてください。答えはページの下にあります。

❶支店に顔を出す。 ➡P103
I ( ) ( ) the ( ) ( ).

❷悪天候で足止めを食う。 ➡P104
I am ( ) ( ) by the bad weather [on my business trip].

❸予算内だと、このホテルしかないかなあ。 ➡P106
This is probably the ( ) hotel ( ) ( ) ( ).

❹滞在時間が2時間、移動時間が8時間の日帰り出張か。疲れるだろうなあ。 ➡P106
It's a ( ) ( ) ( ) with eight hours of traveling for a two-hour visit… I'd be totally ( ) ( ).

❺モーニングコール頼んでおこう。 ➡P110
I'll have to ask for a ( ) ( ).

❻ボードを持った出迎えの人が来てくれてるはずなんだけど、ちゃんと会えるといいなあ。 ➡P110
There is supposed to be someone with a ( ) to ( ) me ( ) here. I hope I can find that person all right.

❼キーパーソンに会えたのは大きな収穫だ。 ➡P112
It was ( ) to meet the ( ) ( ).

❽何とか商談がまとまった。わざわざ来たかいがあったな。 ➡P112
We ( ) to ( ) ( ) ( ). It was ( ) coming ( ) ( ) ( ) here.

❾今回の一番の収穫は、普段見られない、地方の売り場に行けたこと。 ➡P114
The ( ) ( ) ( ) my trip was being able to go to the local shops that I don't usually ( ) ( ) ( ) to see.

❿時差ぼけが抜けないなあ。 ➡P116
I can't ( ) ( ) this ( ) ( ).

---

❶drop/by/branch/office ❷held/up ❸only/within/our/budget ❹one-day/business/trip/worn/out ❺wake-up/call ❻sign/pick/up ❼useful/key/person ❽managed/close/a/deal/worth/all/the/way ❾best/part/of/have/the/chance ❿get/over/jet/lag

chapter 5

企画・開発
Planning & Development

やることも多く、しじゅう頭を
フル回転させているのが
企画・開発のお仕事。
マーケティング調査からアイデア出し、
商品化の実現から広告の手配まで、
一連の流れをたどってみました。

chapter 5 Planning & Development

Words 単語編

❶マーケティング調査
❷アンケート
❸ターゲット
❹ターゲット層
❺ニーズ
❻隙間市場
❼ライバル社
❽トレンド
❾ウェブ広告
❿ユーザー
⓫アフターサービス
⓬口コミ

❶marketing research ❷questionnaire ❸target ❹prospective customers ❺needs ❻niche ❼competitor ❽trend ❾web advertisement ❿end user ⓫after-sales service ⓬word of mouth ⓭draft proposal ⓮budget ⓯cost-benefit performance

まずは、さまざまな物や事の名前で
「企業・開発」のシーンのイメージをつかもう。

⑭予算
⑮費用対効果
⑬企画のたたき台
⑯プロジェクト
⑰商品開発
⑱仕様書
⑲定番商品
⑳パクリ
㉑コンペ
㉒販促
㉓発表会
㉔キャンペーン
㉕リリース資料

⑯project ⑰product development ⑱specifications ⑲staple item ⑳ripoff ㉑competition ㉒sales promotion ㉓press event ㉔campaign ㉕press release

chapter 5 Planning & Development

1 顧客のニーズを探る
We do research on the needs of our clients.

2 マーケティング調査をする
We do marketing research.

3 アンケートを実施する
We do a questionnaire survey.

4 市場ターゲットを定める
We narrow down the target market.

5 身近な相手にヒアリングする
I ask people close to me for their opinions.

tips

❶「〜のニーズに合わせる」は meet/suit one's needs と言う。
❷「調査結果をまとめる」は round up the results of the research。
❸「アンケート結果の集計を取る」は summarize the questionnaire results。questionnaire[kwèstʃənɛ́ər] の発音に注意。
❹「ターゲット市場に合致する」なら fit the target market。

6 ニッチなところを狙う
We target a market niche.

7 他社の動向を調べる
We study the moves of our competitors.

8 ライバル店の視察をする
I go into a competitor's shop.

9 街に出て最近のトレンドを探る
I go to the city to check out the recent trends.

10 企画を通す
I get my plan approved.

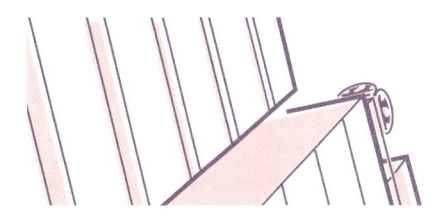

❺「ヒアリング」とは「意見を聞くこと」なのでこのように表現する。hearing とすると「公聴会、尋問」という意味になってしまう。
❻ niche は「隙間市場」の意味。e.g. niche business（隙間産業）
❼ competitor（競合他社）は、単に rival（ライバル）でも OK。
❿「企画を進める」は go on with a plan と言う。

chapter 5 Planning & Development

11 ブレストする
We do some brainstorming.

12 製品を開発する
We develop a product.

13 様々な要素を考慮して価格を設定する
We set prices, taking various aspects into account.

14 コンペを開く
We hold a competition.

15 企画のたたき台を作る
I draw up a draft proposal [for further discussion].

tips

⓫ brainstormは名詞で「ひらめき、インスピレーション」の意味もある。
e.g. have a brainstorm(いい考えを思いつく)
⓭ set the price high(low) とすれば、「価格を高く(低く)設定する」。
⓯「企画のたたき台」は strawman proposal という言い方もある。
⓱ 英語の renew は「[期限など]を更新する」の意味。商品の「リニュー

16 数案に絞り込む
We narrow down our ideas to a few of the best ones.

17 定番商品をリニューアルする
We redesign our staple items.

18 新商品開発に乗り出す
We launch the development of a new product.

19 新機軸を打ち出す
We come out with a breakthrough innovation.

20 費用対効果を計算する
I calculate/assess the cost-benefit performance.

アル」には用いない。「定番商品」はregular <u>items</u>/<u>goods</u>でもOK。
⓲「～に乗り出す」はembark on ～と言ってもよい。
⓳come out withは「[商品]を発表する」、「[アイデア]を打ち出す」の意味。

chapter ❺ Planning & Development

21 予算を立てる
I draw up a budget proposal.

22 予算内に抑える
We keep it within budget.

23 プロジェクトを立ち上げる
We start a new project.

24 スケジュールを組む
I work out a schedule.

25 リスケする
We rearrange our schedule.

tips
㉑「予算を振り分ける」はallocate a budgetと言う。
㉒「予算的に厳しい」はWe are on a tight budget.。
㉔map(計画する)を使ってI map out a schedule.でもよい。
㉕reschedule(リスケする)を使う場合は、後に変更する対象が必要。
e.g. reschedule the meeting(会議の日程を再調整する)

26 仕様書を作る
I draw up specifications.

27 プロジェクトの進捗(ちょく)状況を上司に報告する
I report the progress of the project to my boss.

28 品質検査をする
We test the quality of the product.

29 外部委託する
We outsource jobs.

30 関係各所と調整する
We coordinate with the departments concerned.

㉗「企画の進捗状況はいかがですか？」は、What's the progress on the proposal? または How's the proposal coming along? と言う。
㉙「〜を…に外注する」は <u>outsource</u>/<u>contract out</u> 〜 to … と言う。
㉚「調整役」は coordinating role。e.g. The manager played a coordinating role this time.（今回は部長が調整役を果たした）

chapter 5 Planning & Development

31 自社サイトにウェブ広告を出す
We place an advertisement on our website.

32 販促計画を立てる
I create a plan for promoting sales.

33 他社とコラボする
We collaborate with another company.

34 新製品の発表会を行う
We hold a press event to launch a new product.

35 リリース資料をマスコミ各社に流す
I send out a press release to the media.

tips

㉛「広告を掲載する」はrun an advertisementとも言える。
㉝produce ~ in collaboration with ...で「…とのコラボで~を製作する」。
㉞press eventは「マスコミ向けのイベント・発表会」のこと。
㊱「[商品の]販売経路」はsales outletとも言う。
㊲「紙媒体の広告」はprint advertisement、「電子媒体の広告」は

36 販路を構築する
We develop a distribution channel.

37 広告媒体を決定する
We choose advertising media.

38 広告効果を測定する
We measure advertising effectiveness.

39 新商品発売に合わせてキャンペーンを打つ
We kick off a campaign in conjunction with the product launch.

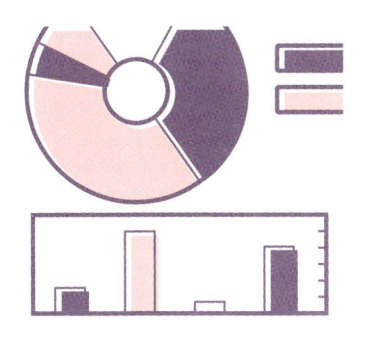

40 広告代理店から相見積を取る
I ask for competitive bids/estimates from several ad agencies.

electronic advertisement と言う。
㊴ kick off はサッカー以外に、「[イベントなど]を開始する」の意味でもよく使う。in conjunction with ~ は「~と連動して」。
㊵「相見積」は単に bids あるいは estimates でも OK。

chapter 5 Planning & Development

1 この市場は、ほんと混戦模様だな。
There really is a rat race going on in the market.

---

2 最近のユーザーは賢いから、企業に簡単に踊らされたりしない。
End users these days are too smart to be manipulated easily by big businesses.

---

3 今までの成功体験は全部捨てよう。
Let's forget all the successful experiences we've had before now.

---

4 もっとユーザー視点に立たないと。
It's better to reflect the needs of the users.

---

5 一体、この商品のターゲット層はどこなの?
Who the hell is this product targeted at?

---

6 これからはシニア層も視野に入れないとね。
We're going to also have to take the senior market into account.

rat race = 過酷な生存競争／go on = 続く、進行する

rat race はネズミの行動（同じ動作を繰り返すが疲れるだけで何も得ない）に由来。「混戦状態」は scramble とも言う。e.g. There's a mad scramble in the cellphone market.（携帯電話市場は混戦状態だ）

---

end user = 末端の利用者、エンドユーザー／too ~ to ... = あまりに~なので…できない／be manipulated = 操られる／big business = 大企業

「~をもてあそぶ」は play cat and mouse with ~。e.g. Big businesses sometimes seem to be playing cat and mouse with customers.（大企業は時として消費者をもてあそんでいるように思える）

---

forget = 忘れる（つまり「捨てる」）／successful = うまくいった

「初心に帰る」は go back to basics。e.g. Let's go back to basics and look at the project with a fresh eye.（初心に戻って新鮮な目で計画を見直そう）

It's better to ~ = もっと~しないと、した方がよい／reflect = 熟考する、よく考える

「人の身になってみる」は put oneself in someone's shoes と言う。e.g. You have to put yourself in the customers' shoes.（顧客の立場になってみないと）

Who the hell ~? = 一体全体、誰が~のか（かなりくだけた言い方）

サービスやイベントなどが「~向けの、~対象の」は、be intended for ~。e.g. This PC workshop is intended for beginners who need typing skills.（このパソコンワークショップはタイピングスキルを必要とする初心者が対象です）

---

take ~ into account = ~を考慮に入れる

動詞 eye（視野に入れる）を使って、eye the senior market と言ってもよい。「市場を拡大・拡張する」は expand/enlarge the market と言う。

chapter 5 Planning & Development

7 主婦から集めた正直な生の声を商品開発に生かそう。
Let's make good use of the real <u>voices</u>/<u>opinions</u> collected from housewives for product development.

8 このデータって古いよね？ 最近のはないんだっけ？
That is the old data, isn't it? Don't we have the latest data?

9 顧客が反応するツボって、たまに理解不能。
Sometimes I have no idea what gets the customer hooked.

10 売上も利益も昨対比をクリアしてる！
Great! We've gained more sales and earnings than last year.

11 お、そのネタ使えそう。いただき！
Oh, that's a good idea. I'm going to call it mine.

12 要するに、思いつきだけの企画って、結局実現しないんだよ。
Basically, random ideas often end up going up in smoke.

make good use of ~ = ～を活用する／product development = 商品開発

「アイデアを新製品開発に生かす」は、develop the idea into a new product。「[消費者に] 商品に関するアンケート調査をする」は <u>do</u>/<u>conduct</u> a questionnaire survey on the product と言うことができる。

Don't we ~ =[私たちは]～ではなかった?／latest = 最新の

latest の late は「最近の」の意味。「更新されたデータ」は updated data、「修正されたデータ」は revised data と言う。「データを廃棄する」は destroy data。e.g. Please destroy the data after reading it. (読み終わったらデータを廃棄してください)。

---

get ~ hooked = ～を釘づけにする、夢中にさせる

「世の中何が売れるかわからない」は、We never know what will be in. と言う。in は「流行している、人気がある」という意味の形容詞。

---

gain = 獲得する／earnings = 事業利益(通常複数)

「昨対比、前年比」は compared to <u>last year</u> / <u>the previous year</u> でもよい。e.g. Our income has grown 5 percent compared to last year. (当社の収益は昨対比5パーセントの成長を遂げた)

---

call ~ mine = ～を自分のものと呼ぶ、自分のものにする

「面白い(笑える)ネタがある」は I have a funny story. でよい。「ゴシップネタ」は gossip fodder、「下ネタ」は dirty joke と言う。また「[小説や映画の] ネタバレ」は spoiler と言い、ネット上ではしばしば Spoiler Warning (ネタバレ注意) の注意書きが見られる。

---

basically = 基本的に、要するに／random = でたらめの／end up ~ing = 結果的に～になる／go up in smoke = 水泡に帰す、おじゃんになる

「思いつきで」は off the top of one's head (頭のてっぺんから出た) を使って、The idea is just off the top of my head. (そのアイデアは単なる思いつきです) と言うことができる。

chapter 5 Planning & Development

13 その企画、すっごく斬新なんですけど、まだ時代がそこまで追いついていないっていうか……。
I know how original your idea is but it seems a bit too far out for the current times.

---

14 独創的なんだけど、非現実的なんだよね。
I must say your idea sounds unique, but far-fetched as well.

---

15 たいした企画書じゃなくてもパワポだとよく見える。
PowerPoint makes your proposal look better even if it's not a big deal.

---

16 彼女の企画の方がキャッチーだよ。
Her proposal looks more attractive.

---

17 この企画もボツか。目下４連敗中だよ。
I got my proposal turned down again. This is the fourth time in a row.

---

18 パイを作るのか奪うのか、まずそこから決めないと。
We should start off by deciding whether we'll create need or grab market share.

original = 創意に富む、新奇な／far out = 現実離れした、斬新すぎる／current times = 現代

「[良い意味で] 時代を先取りしている」は be ahead of the times。e.g. The fuel supply system is ahead of the times.（その燃料供給システムは時代を先取りしている）

I must say ~ = ~と言わざるを得ない／far-fetched = とっぴな

far-fetched の "fetch" は「持ってくる」という意味。「遠くから持ってくる」つまり「とっぴな、非現実的な」。類義語としては unrealistic（非現実的な）が一般的だが、off-the-wall（「壁から外れた」＝「とっぴな」）という口語的な表現もある。

---

not a big deal = 大ごとではない、たいしたことない

It's not a big deal.（たいしたことないよ）は依頼やお願いに対する返答でも使われる。e.g. "Can you fix this chair?"（いす直してくれる？）→ "It's not a big deal."（朝飯前だよ）

---

attractive = 魅力的、引きつける力がある

catchy は英語で「覚えやすい、人に受ける」の意味。e.g. catchy tune（覚えやすい曲）、catchy packaging（人目を引くパッケージ）。この文脈では attractive（魅力的な）または appealing（人に訴えかける）の方が意味的に近い。

---

get ~ turned down = ~を却下される／in a row = 続けて、連続で

「不採用になる」は reject を使って、get ~ rejected とも言える。「採用する」は adopt。e.g. Finally, my proposal got adopted.（ついに企画が採用された）

---

start off by ~ing = ~することから始める／whether ~ = ~かどうか／grab = 獲得する、ひったくる

英語での pie（パイ）は「全体、総額」の意味。e.g. Axcellor Inc. takes a big share of the online advertising pie.（アクセラー社はオンライン広告全体の中で大きな割合を占めている）

chapter 5 Planning & Development

19 ワンアイデアだけで引っ張っていくには無理がある。
We can't go on with this plan with just a single idea.

20 スポンサー受けのいい企画だね。
That idea should sound appealing to our sponsors.

21 リピーターが大切だから、アフターサービスを充実させないと。
We should provide better after-sale service to encourage return customers.

22 なんか最近企画がマンネリ化してるなあ。
I'm stuck in a rut when it comes to getting new ideas.

23 女心をくすぐる車って、どんなの?
I wonder what type of car stirs women's emotions.

24 やっぱりオッさんの発想には限界があるね。
You know there's a limit to what an old man can think of.

go on with ~ = ～をどんどん進める

go further/press on with ~（～を推し進める）を使ってもよい。e.g. The local government pressed on with the construction of the disposal facility.（地方自治体はごみ処理施設の建設計画を推し進めた）

---

appeal to ~ = ～に訴えかける、アピールする

be received well by ~ でも「～に受けがいい」の意味になる。e.g. Your presentation was received well by the audience.（君の発表、聴衆に受けがよかったよ）

---

after-sale service = アフターサービス／encourage = 促進する、奨励する／return customer = 常連客、リピーター

アフターサービス、リピーターはともに和製英語なので注意。「大切な顧客」は valued customer と言う。

---

be stuck in a rut = マンネリになる／when it comes to ~ = ～のことになると

「[生活・仕事が] 単調な、マンネリの」は humdrum。e.g I got bored with the humdrum nine-to-five routine.（9時5時のマンネリの仕事に飽きた）

---

stir = 刺激する、感激させる／emotion = 感情

「女心」は woman's feelings/mind とも言う。e.g. You don't understand women's feelings.（女心のわからない人ね）、A woman's mind and a winter wind change oft.（＜ことわざ＞女心と秋の空）

You know = ほら、やっぱり／old man = おじさん（「老人」の意味にもなる）

「頭の固い人、保守的な人」を軽蔑して stick in the mud と言うことも。My boss is such a stick in the mud.（うちの上司はほんと頭が固い）。

chapter ❺ Planning & Development

25 ろくなアイデアが出ないな。もっと外に出て刺激を受けないと。
I never get any good ideas. I should go out more often and get some inspiration.

---

26 ちょっとぉ、これってうちのパクリじゃないの?
Hey, isn't this a ripoff of our product?

---

27 あ〜やられた! マグノックス社の新商品、ちょっと先を越されちゃったって感じ。
Darn! The recent product of Magnox is just one step ahead of us, isn't it?

---

28 もっとよく練れば、もしかすると化けるかも。
This idea could turn out to be something if we keep working on it.

---

29 ここらでヒットを出さないと、うちの部署、次がないよ。
The department has no future unless we produce a hit right now.

---

30 このプロジェクトには、企画段階から参加してるから思い入れがある。
I have a special attachment to the project because I've been working on it since the planning stage.

inspiration = 刺激、ひらめき、インスピレーション

「アイデアを思いつく」は come up with an idea、「アイデアをひねり出す」は squeeze out an idea。「気分転換に外出する」は go outside for a change と言う。

---

ripoff = 盗作、パクリ

ripoff は「暴利、ぼったくり」の意味でもしばしば使われる。e.g. This hamburger is $30? It's a ripoff.（このハンバーガーが 30 ドル？ ぼったくりだよ）

Darn = まいった、やられた／one step ahead of ~ = ~の一歩先を行く

他に one step（一歩）を使った表現としては、We are left one step behind.（当社は後手に回っている）、You can do it one step at a time.（少しずつやっていいですよ）がある。

---

turn out to be ~ = 結果的に~になる／something = 大したもの／work on ~ = ~に取り組む

この something は、The new boss is really something.（新しく来た上司は大した人物だ）、Isn't that something?（それはすごいことですよね）のように使われる名詞。

---

unless ~ = もし~でなければ／produce a hit = ヒット作を出す

「土壇場に追い込まれる」は be driven into a ditch、または、have one's back against the wall と言う。e.g. Due to the cancellation of the big project, we had our backs against the wall.（一大プロジェクトの中止が決定され、当社は窮地に立たされた）

---

special attachment to ~ = ~への特別な思い入れ、愛着／planning stage = 企画段階

「~に深い愛着を持っている」は be deeply attached to ~。e.g. I'm deeply attached to this department.（この部署に深い愛着がある）

chapter 5 Planning & Development

31 明日のコンペに間に合わないと、今までの努力がすべてパーだ。
All my efforts will go right down the drain if I can't make it to the competition tomorrow.

32 前回のコンペの敗因を調査して、次回のコンペに生かそう。
I'm going to study why I lost in the last competition so I won't lose in the next one.

33 このアイデア／プランならきっといける！
This idea/plan is sure to get the green light.

34 この案を通すのが、入社以来の夢だったんだ！
It's been my dream to get this proposal approved since I joined the company.

35 いつか、億単位のプロジェクトを動かしてみたいなあ。
I wish I could run a hundred-million-yen project some time in the future.

36 価格競争が激しくなってきた。
Price competition is getting severe.

go down the drain = 水の泡になる／make it to ~ = ~に間に合う／competition = コンペ、コンテスト

make it to ~ は概して否定語とともに使われる表現。「~に参加する」の意味でもよく使われる。e.g. I couldn't make it to the meeting because of the train delay.（電車が遅れて会議に参加できなかった）

---

study = 調べる／so ~ not ... = ~が…しないために

「~しないように」は so as not to ~、in order not to ~ なども使える。e.g. so as not to repeat the mistake（過ちを繰り返さないように）

---

get the green light = 許可、ゴーサインをもらう

「ゴーサインをもらう」は get the go-ahead とも言う。「却下される」は get shot down。e.g. My proposal got shot down in the first stage.（僕の企画は第1段階で却下された）

---

get ~ approved = ~を承認してもらう／join the company = 入社する cf. join = ~に入る

「[企画など]を受け入れる（断る）」は say yes(no) to ~。e.g. It's easy to say no to a project and it's hard to say yes.（企画を断るのは簡単だが、受け入れるのは難しい）

I wish I could ~ = ~できたらなあ、~できたらいいのに／run = 運営する／some time = いつか

run の意外な意味としてはほかに「[広告]を掲載する」、「[費用]がかかる」がある。e.g. We're going to run an ad in the newspaper.（新聞広告を出す予定です）、e.g. The installation of the device will run you $200.（装置の設置には200ドルかかります）

---

price competition(= price war) = 価格[破壊]競争／severe = 容赦ない

「価格競争力のある[低価格の]商品」は competitively-priced product。e.g. Generally, customers want a high-quality but competitively-priced product.（一般的に消費者は品質が高く、他社に比べて安い商品を求める）

chapter ❺ Planning & Development

37 こんなにコストがかかるんじゃ経営陣を説得できないよ。
I doubt we can convince the executives to go ahead with this when the costs are that high.

---

38 これじゃ売れるほど赤字が増えていっちゃうじゃないか。
Hey, that means the more we sell, the more of a deficit we'll be suffering from.

---

39 予算を考えると、なんだかアイデアもしぼんでいく感じ。
With such a small budget in mind, I can't help running low on ideas.

---

40 営業は勝手なこと言うけど、実現するのがどんだけ大変かわかってるのかね。
Sales staff say whatever they want, but they don't realize how hard it is to bring the idea together.

---

41 品質には自信あるんだけど、デザインについては何というか……。
I'm 100 percent sure of the quality. But I don't know what to say when it comes to the design.

---

42 クオリティーはもちろん大事だけど、納期に間に合わなかったら意味無いんだよ。
True, quality is important, but it doesn't mean a thing if you can't meet the deadline.

I doubt ~ = ～を疑わしく思う、～とは思えない／**convince ~ to ...** = ～に…するよう説得する／**executives** = 経営陣／**go ahead with ~** = [計画など]を進める／**when ~** = ～だと言うのに（譲歩・対照のニュアンス）

win ~ over も「～を説得する」の意味で使われる言い方。e.g. I wonder if I can win my boss over to give me a raise.（給料を上げてもらえるよううまく上司を説得できるかな）

---

that means ~ = それでは～ということになる／**the more ~, the more ...** = ～すればするほど…する／**deficit** = 赤字／**suffer from ~** = ～で苦しむ

「赤字である」は have a deficit、または、in the red と言う。「黒字」は in the black。e.g. The company keeps running in the red.（その会社は赤字経営を続けている）

---

with ~ in mind = ～が心にあると、～だと思うと／**can't help ~ing** = ～せずにはいられない／**run low on ~** = ～が乏しくなる

逆にアイデアがわく場合は、turn on the light bulb（電球をつける、ひらめく）という表現がある。e.g. A brief talk with an engineer turned on the light bulb in my mind.（エンジニアとの短い会話でアイデアがひらめいた）

---

whatever they want [to say] = [言い]たいことはどんなことでも／**bring ~ together** = ～をまとめる、形にする

ビジネスでは、「実現可能な」は realize（実現する）の形容詞 realizable 以外に、feasible もよく使われる。e.g. feasible plan(technology/product)（実現可能な計画＜技術／製品＞）

---

be 100 percent sure of ~ = ～を100パーセント確信している／**when it comes to ~** = ～のこととなると、～について言うと

大事なことに関して「お茶を濁す」は dodge the subject。e.g. My supervisor dodges the subject when it comes to my job advancement.（昇進の話になると上司はお茶を濁す）

[It is] true ~ but ... = 確かに～だけど…／**not mean a thing** = 何の意味も無い／**meet the deadline** = 締切に間に合わせる

「～締切の」は due。"When is that due?"（締切はいつ？）、"The report is due [on] next Monday."（その報告書は来週の月曜が締切日だ）

chapter 5 Planning & Development

43 さすがに3カ月じゃ無理だって。
How come they expect me to get this done in three months? It's impossible.

---

44 大事なのはチームワークだから。
What counts most is teamwork, you know.

---

45 はあ、今日も徹夜だあ。
Whew ... I'm going to have to work through the night again.

---

46 もうちょっと販促に予算が回せたらなあ。
If only we could have a bigger budget for sales promotion.

---

47 ユーザー属性を考えてターゲットに刺さるコピーを考えなきゃね。
We should take the users' perspectives into account and come up with a slogan that sticks in their minds.

---

48 この商品のターゲット層には、ファッション誌への広告が有効かな。
I assume placing an ad in fashion magazines will be effective for the prospective customers.

How come ~? = どうして〜なのですか（非難のニュアンス）／expect ~ to ... = 〜に…するよう期待する／get ~ done = 〜を終わらせる、仕上げる

「無理だ」は beyond one's power（力の限界を超えて）を使って、Getting this done in three months is beyond my power.（3 カ月でこれを仕上げるのは自分の限界を超えている）とも表現できる。

---

what counts is ~ = 重要なことは〜／you know = 〜ですよね

Teamwork is everything.（チームワークがすべて）、Teamwork is what it takes to win.（チームワークは勝つために必要なことだ）と言ってもよい。what it takes to ~ は「〜するのに必要なこと、欠かせないこと」。

Whew = ふう、やれやれ／through the night = 夜通しで

「徹夜する」には pull an all-nighter という表現もある。e.g. I pulled an all-nighter yesterday and finished the quarterly report.（昨日は徹夜して四半期報告書を仕上げたよ）

---

if only ~ = 〜でさえあればなあ／sales promotion = 販売促進

be on a tight budget で「予算が厳しい」。e.g. We can't afford to hire new staff because we are on a tight budget.（会社は予算が厳しいので新人を雇う余裕がない）

---

take ~ into account = 〜を考慮する／perspective = 視点、観点／come up with ~ = 〜を考え出す／slogan = コピー／stick in ~ = 〜にずっと残る

「心に残る」は have a good hook（引き付けるものがある）を使っても表現できる。e.g. We need a background story that has a good hook.（人を引き付けるような背景となる話が必要だ）

---

assume = 仮定する、想定する／place an ad = 広告を出す／effective = 有効な／prospective customer = 見込み客

prospective の元となる prospect も「見込み客、潜在顧客」という意味でよく使われる単語。e.g. We expect that millions of target prospects will visit our website.（何百万人もの見込み客が当社ウェブサイトを閲覧するだろうと予想している）

chapter ❺ Planning & Development

49 発行部数の一番多い新聞に広告を出そうよ。

What do you say to running an ad in the largest circulating paper?

---

50 ウェブはうまく使わないと逆効果だよ。

The website can have a negative effect on sales if you don't use it properly.

---

51 バナー広告のクリック率を上げるにはどうしたらいいんだろう？

I wonder what I should do to raise the click-rate of our banner ad.

---

52 なんのかんの言って、テレビの威力はばかにできない。

No matter what you say, you can't underestimate the impact TV has.

---

53 やっぱり口コミが一番効くな。

Word of mouth definitely works wonders.

run an ad = 広告を打つ／circulating = 発行されている

What do you say to ~ing? は、相手の意見を尋ねたり、相手を誘うときに使う表現。前者であればWhat do you think of ~?（~をどう思いますか）、後者であれば How about ~ing?（~はどうですか）が同様の表現。

---

negative effect on ~ = ~へのマイナス効果／properly = 適切に

「逆効果」は adverse/reverse effect でもよい。e.g. Working out too much can have an adverse effect on your health.（トレーニングしすぎると健康には逆効果だよ）

---

click-rate = クリック率／banner ad = バナー広告

「うっとうしいバナー広告」は annoying banner ad と言う。e.g. I don't know how to prevent these annoying banner ads.（どうやったらこのバナー広告を防ぐことができるのかわからない）

---

no matter what ~ = どんなことを~でも、どんなに~したところで／underestimate = 低く見積もる、みくびる／impact = 影響力、効果

the impact TV has は the powerful grip of TV（強力なテレビの影響）とも言える。なお、gripping は「人を魅了する」という意味の形容詞。e.g. a gripping story of genetic engineering（興味深い遺伝子工学の話）

---

word of mouth = 口コミ／work wonders = 驚くほど効果がある

「口コミで~を宣伝する」は promote ~ by word of mouth。「口コミで広まる」は spread through word of mouth、「~に関する口コミ情報」は word-of-mouth information on ~ と言う。

Skit 企画開発編

企画はパス？ ボツ？ 明暗分けたプランナー二人

Man: **I heard[1] you're going to** start a new project.
Woman: It's been my dream to get the proposal approved since I joined the company.
M: I'm stuck in a rut when it comes to getting new ideas. **How did you do it?**
W: **I did marketing research** and a questionnaire survey to target a market niche.
M: **Susan's** proposal looked more attractive, **but you had a better idea.**
W: **Thanks, but now there's a lot to do. I have to** draw up specifications **and** work out a schedule, **and I have to** keep it within budget.
M: **I got my proposal turned down again. This is the fourth time in a row.**
W: **That's too bad[2].** You should go out more often to get some inspiration.

男性：新しいプロジェクトを立ち上げるって聞いたけど。
女性：入社以来、企画を通すのが、私の夢だったの。
男：僕なんか、最近企画がマンネリ化しててさあ。一体どうやったの？
女：ニッチなところを狙おうと思って、マーケティング調査をしたり、アンケートをとったり。
男：スーザンの企画の方が、魅力的には見えたけど、アイデアは君のが上だったよ。
女：ありがとう。でも今度はやることが山ほどあるのよ。仕様書作ったり、スケジュール組んだり。しかも予算内で抑えなきゃなんないし。
男：僕の方は、また企画がボツで、目下4連敗中だよ。
女：それは残念ねえ。もっと外に出て、刺激を受けてみたらいいんじゃない。

【語注】

❶ I hear ~: ～だそうだ、～だと聞いている
❷ That's too bad.: それは残念だ。お気の毒だ。

Quick Check

本章に出てきたフレーズを復習しましょう。以下の日本語の意味になるよう英文を完成させてください。答えはページの下にあります。

❶ 様々な要素を考慮して価格を設定する。 ➡P128
We set prices, (　　　) various (　　　)(　　　)(　　　).

❷ 新機軸を打ち出す。 ➡P129
We (　　　)(　　　)(　　　) a (　　　) innovation.

❸ 新商品発売に合わせてキャンペーンを打つ。 ➡P133
We (　　　)(　　　) a campaign (　　　)(　　　)(　　　) the product (　　　).

❹ 要するに思いつきだけの企画って、結局実現しないんだよ。 ➡P136
Basically, (　　　) ideas often end up (　　　) up in (　　　).

❺ 明日のコンペに間に合わないと、今までの努力がすべてパーだ。 ➡P144
All my efforts will (　　　) right (　　　)(　　　)(　　　) if I can't make it to the competition tomorrow.

❻ このアイデア／プランならきっといける！ ➡P144
This idea/plan is sure to (　　　) the (　　　)(　　　).

❼ 予算を考えると、なんだかアイデアもしぼんでいく感じ。 ➡P146
With such a (　　　) budget (　　　)(　　　), I can't help (　　　)(　　　)(　　　) ideas.

❽ 品質には自信あるんだけど、デザインについては何というか……。 ➡P146
I'm (　　　)(　　　)(　　　) of the quality. But I don't know what to say (　　　)(　　　)(　　　)(　　　) the design.

❾ 大事なのはチームワークだから。 ➡P148
(　　　)(　　　)(　　　) is teamwork, you know.

❿ やっぱり口コミが一番効くな。 ➡P150
(　　　)(　　　)(　　　) definitely (　　　)(　　　).

---

❶ taking/aspects/into/account　❷ come/out/with/breakthrough　❸ kick/off/in/conjunction/with/launch　❹ random/going/smoke　❺ go/down/the/drain　❻ get/green/light　❼ small/in/mind/running/low/on　❽ 100/percent/sure/when/it/comes/to　❾ What/counts/most　❿ Word/of/mouth/works/wonders

chapter 6
休憩
Taking a Break

缶コーヒーを飲んで休憩したり、
お昼休みにランチに連れ立ったり、
給湯室でうわさ話に花を咲かせたり――
オフィスライフを送る人々が
一息入れるさまざまなシーンでの
行動や心模様です。

chapter 6 Taking a Break

Words 単語編

❶ ひと休み
❷ 息抜き、休憩
❸ 休憩室
❹ 自販機
❺ 購買
❻ 喫煙所
❼ ヘビースモーカー
❽ 目薬
❾ 給湯室
❿ うわさ話
⓫ 昼休み
⓬ 社員食堂
⓭ 食堂
⓮ 食堂街
⓯ 日替わりランチ
⓰ A定食
⓱ 立ち食いそば

❶breather ❷break ❸staff room ❹vending machine ❺company shop ❻smoking area ❼heavy smoker ❽eyedrops ❾staff kitchen ❿gossip ⓫lunchtime ⓬company cafeteria ⓭

まずは、さまざまな物や事の名前で
「休憩」のシーンのイメージをつかもう。

⑳ATM
㉑屋上
㉒洗面所、化粧室
㉓化粧
⑲公共料金
⑱用事
㉔おやつ
㉕昼寝、居眠り

restaurant/diner ⑭restaurant arcade ⑮daily lunch special ⑯A meal-set ⑰soba at a stand-up counter ⑱errand ⑲utility bill ⑳cash machine ㉑rooftop ㉒restroom ㉓makeup ㉔snack ㉕nap

chapter 6 Taking a Break

1 お茶を飲んで一息つく
I take a breather over a cup of tea.

2 自販機(購買)で飲み物を買う
I get a drink <u>from the vending machine (at the company shop)</u>.

3 休憩室で一服する
I have a smoke in the staff room.

4 目薬をさす
I put in some eyedrops.

5 同僚と社食にランチに行く
I go for lunch at the company cafeteria with my colleague[s].

tips

❶breather は「息抜き、一休み」、take a breather で「一息つく、休憩する」。I have a tea break. と言ってもよい。
❸「食後の一服」なら after-meal cigarette、「一服(一休み)しよう」なら Let's have a break.。
❻「行列を避けるために…」なら ... to avoid a long line。

6 混むのを避けて時間差で昼食に出かける
I shift my lunch hour to avoid the crowd.

7 ランチに隣駅まで足を伸ばす
I go all the way to the next station to have lunch.

8 電話番を交替してもらう
I ask someone else to handle the phone calls [while I'm gone/out].

9 お昼に出前を頼む
I have my lunch delivered.

10 散歩して息抜きする
I take a walk for a change.

❼ go all the way to ~ は「わざわざ~へ行く」。
❽ handle は「~に対処する、~を担当する」。
❾ have ~ delivered で「~を配達してもらう」という意味。
❿ for a change は「気分転換に、息抜きに」。I take a walk and relax. と言ってもよい。

chapter 6 Taking a Break

11 午後のハードワークに備えて英気を養う
I rest, and get my energy back for the tough work [to come] in the afternoon.

12 軽く昼寝をする
I take a quick nap.

13 机につっぷして寝る
I rest my head on the desk and take a nap.

14 昼休みに用事をすませる
I get my errands done during my lunch break.

15 ATMで今晩の飲み会のお金を下ろす
I get some money out from the cash machine for tonight's after-work drink.

tips

⓫ tough work は「きつい、大変な仕事」。
⓬ nap は「うたた寝、昼寝」。
⓭ take a nap の代わりに sleep と言ってもよい。
⓮ errand は「用事」。「用事をすませる」は I finish what I have to do.（やるべきことを終える）と言ってもよい。

16 歯磨きと化粧直しをする
I brush my teeth and freshen up my makeup.

17 おやつ休憩をする
I take a [short] break to have a snack.

18 3時のおやつを配る(食べる)
I pass out (eat) afternoon snacks.

19 給湯室で井戸端会議(おしゃべり)をする
I stand around gossiping(chatting) with co-workers in the staff kitchen.

⑮ATMはautomated teller machineの略。cash machineとも言う。
⑯「化粧直しをする」はreapply my makeupと言い換えられる。
⑱pass out(配る)はhand outでも同じ。
⑲stand around ~ingで「立って~する」。単にI gossip/chat with co-workersと言ってもよい。

chapter 6 Taking a Break

1. 切りのいいところで休憩取ってね。
[Please] take a break when things have settled down a bit.

2. たまには息抜きしてください。
You deserve a break from time to time.

3. しょっちゅう目を休ませとかないと[PCの]画面の見過ぎで眼精疲労になるよ。
You should rest your eyes frequently, or you will strain your eyes from staring at the computer screen for too long.

4. 雲隠れしたと思ったら、彼女トイレで眠ってたわ。
She suddenly disappeared, taking a nap in the restroom.

5. 眠気ざましにコーヒーでも入れよう。
I'll get a cup of coffee to wake me up.

6. 最近は煙草を吸える場所を見つけるのにも一苦労だ。
Nowadays I have trouble finding places where smoking is not prohibited.

take a break = 休憩する、一休みする／**things have settled down** = 事態が落ち着いた cf. settle down = 落ち着く／**a bit** = 少し、ちょっと

「切りのいいところで」は when you think it's OK to stop what you are doing（作業を中断していいと思うときに）とも言える。

---

deserve = 〜がふさわしい、〜して当然だ／**break** = 休み、休憩／**from time to time** = 時々、時たま

You need to relax once in a while.（たまには息抜きしないと）と言ってもよい。

---

rest = 休ませる／**frequently** = 頻繁に、しばしば／**strain** = 使いすぎて痛める cf. eyestrain = 眼精疲労／**stare at ~** = 〜を見つめる、／**computer screen** = コンピューター画面

You will get eyestrain if you keep staring at the computer screen.（画面を見続けると目が疲れるよ）でも同じ。

---

suddenly = 突然／**disappear** = 見えなくなる、姿を消す／**take a nap** = うたた寝する、仮眠を取る／**restroom** = 化粧室、洗面所、トイレ cf. bathroom = トイレ

前半は、She was suddenly nowhere in sight（急にどこにも見当たらなくなった）と言うこともできる。

---

get a cup of coffee = コーヒーを一杯持ってくる、入れる／**wake ~ up** = 〜の目をさます、起こす

get はコーヒーを自分で入れる場合も買う場合も使える。「眠気を防ぐ（目を覚ましておく）ためにコーヒーでも沸かそう」なら I'll make some coffee to keep myself awake. となる。

---

nowadays = 最近では、近頃／**have trouble ~ing** = 〜するのに苦労する／**not prohibited** = 禁止されていない cf. prohibit = 禁止する

Nowadays it's very difficult to find places where I can smoke.（煙草を吸える場所を見つけるのは大変だ）と言い換えられる。

chapter 6 Taking a Break

7 彼はヘビースモーカーだから、喫煙所にいる時間の方が長いんじゃない?

I think he hangs around in the smoking area much longer than in the office because he's such a heavy smoker.

8 今日はお給料日だから、ランチ奮発しちゃおうよ!

It's payday, so let's eat something nice for lunch!

9 珍しく上司からランチに誘われた。こりゃあ、なんかあるな。

My boss asked me out for lunch, which is very rare. I suspect there must be something up with him.

10 いつもの店は飽きたから、今日は別の店に行こうかな。

I'm rather tired of the usual restaurant, so I may try a different one today.

11 どこも込んでて、ランチ難民になっちゃう。

Every place is so crowded that maybe I won't get to eat my lunch!

12 この列に並んでたら昼休みが終わっちゃうよ!

If I wait in line here, my lunch break will be over!

hang around = うろつく、たむろする／**smoking area** = 喫煙場所 cf. non-smoking area = 禁煙場所／**much longer than ~** = ～よりもずっと長く／**smoker** = 喫煙者 cf. I'm a smoker. = 私はたばこを吸います

「禁煙する、たばこをやめる」は <u>quit</u>/<u>stop</u>/<u>give up</u> smoking。

---

payday = 給料日 cf. pay = 支払い、給料／**eat something nice** = 何かおいしいものを食べる

「ランチを奮発する」は eat something special for lunch でもよい。「豪勢なランチ（食事）」は splendid <u>lunch</u>(<u>meal</u>)。

---

ask ~ out for ... = ～を…に誘う cf. ask ~ out for a date = ～をデートに誘う／**rare** = めったにない、珍しい／**I suspect** = ～ではないかと思う、疑う／**be something up** = 何かがある

この which は My boss asked me out for lunch = 上司が自分をランチに誘ったこと全体を受けている。

---

be tired of ~ = ～に飽き飽きする cf. be fed up with ~ = ～にうんざりする／**usual** = いつもの、普段の／**a different one** = 違うもの（この one は restaurant を指す）

I've had enough of the usual restaurant, so I may try a new one today.（いつもの店はもう十分なので今日は新しい店を試してみよう）とも言える。

---

every place = どの場所も（**every ~** は単数扱い、動詞は **is**）／**crowded** = 混雑した／**not get to eat ~** = ～を食べ損ねる

前半は、All the restaurants are so crowded（飲食店はどこも込んでいる）としてもよい。「ランチ難民」は（×）lunch refugee と直訳しても通じないので、「お昼を食べ損ねる」としている。

---

wait in line = 列に並んで待つ cf. in line = 一列になって／**lunch break** = 昼休み cf. lunch hour でも同じ／**be over** = 終わる

wait in line の代わりに stand in line（列を作る、並ぶ）と言ってもよい。

chapter 6 Taking a Break

13 デザートまで付いてこの値段？ ここの日替わりランチ、相当お得だ。
This price includes dessert? The daily lunch special at this restaurant is really reasonable.

14 もうかなり待たされてるけど、私のA定食はまだかな？
I've been waiting for so long, but my A meal-set still isn't here yet.

15 お昼代500円しかもらってないから、100円バーガー、まじ助かる。
I only have 500 yen for lunch, so 100-yen burgers are really helpful.

16 立ち食いそば、わびしいなあ。
It's really dreary to eat *soba* at a stand-up counter.

17 やばっ。ネクタイにラーメンの汁飛ばしちゃった。
Oops! I splashed the noodle soup on my tie!

18 バランスよく食べたいから、ランチは手作りしてます。
I make my lunch so that I can eat a well-balanced meal.

include = 含める／**dessert** = デザート／**daily lunch special** = 日替わり定食 cf. daily = 毎日の／**reasonable** = 手頃な、お値打ち価格の cf. cheap = 安い、安っぽい｜inexpensive = 高くない

前半は Is dessert included in the price? や The meal includes dessert at this price? と言ってもよい。

---

for so long = 長いこと、ずっと／**A meal-set** = A定食 cf. set meal = 定食｜combo meal＝ファストフード店のセット／**still isn't here yet** = まだ来ていない cf. stillもyetも「まだ」という意味

「お昼に定食を食べる」と言うなら I have a set meal for lunch.。

---

burger = バーガー、ハンバーガー cf. hamburger = ハンバーガー｜Give me a burger and fries.＝ハンバーガーとフライドポテトをください／**helpful** = 助けになる

ファストフードと言えば、英語で「マクドナルド」＝ McDonald's は「マック（mac）」などとは省略しないので注意。

---

dreary = わびしい、もの悲しい／**soba** = そば cf.英語で説明するなら「そば」は buckwheat noodle、「うどん」は wheat noodle／**stand-up** = 立ったままの

It brings me down to eat soba at a stand-up counter.（立ち食いそばを食べるとわびしくなる）とも言える。

Oops! = おっと!、しまった!／**splash** = [液体]を散らす、飛ばす／cf.「ラーメン、中華麺」はramen、Chinese noodles｜「即席麺」はinstant noodle／**tie** = ネクタイ

Oh, no! I stained my tie with a noodle soup splash!（おっと！ ネクタイをラーメンの汁で汚してしまった！）でもよい。stain は「染みをつける」。

---

make one's lunch = 自分の昼食を作る／**eat a meal** = 食事をする cf. have a mealも同じ／**well-balanced meal** = バランスの取れた食事

ほかに I do my best to eat well-balanced meals, so I make my lunch [every day]. や I want to eat healthy, so I prepare my lunch. で言い換えが可能。

chapter 6 Taking a Break

19 今日は天気がいいから、屋上でお弁当食べようかな。
It's such a nice day! I'd like to have lunch on the rooftop [of the office building].

20 愛妻弁当なんてうらやましい!
You are so lucky to have a wife who packs your lunch [every day]!

21 ほんとは一人でランチしたいんだけど付き合いあるし……。
Actually, I'd like to have lunch by myself, but I have to socialize with others…

22 仕事の話をしながら食べると消化に悪いよ。
It's not good for digestion if you talk about work while eating.

23 お昼休みは貴重な情報交換の場だよね。
Lunch hour is a great time to exchange information [, don't you think?]

24 あの気になるニュース、今のうちにネットでチェックしとこうかな。
Maybe I should check out that interesting news on the Net right now.

It's such a nice day! = とても気持ちのいい日だ! cf. What a nice day!でも同じ／**I'd like to ~** = ～したいと思う／**rooftop** = 屋上 cf. 単にroofでも可

「いい天気」は nice day のほかに sunny day（晴れた日）、beautiful day（素晴らしい天気の日）などとも言える。

---

lucky to have ~ = ～がいてくれるのはいいことだ、運がいい／**pack one's lunch** = 弁当を詰める、作る cf. prepare one's lunch（弁当を用意する）でも可

I envy you for having a lunch your wife prepared for you!（奥さんが用意してくれた弁当なんてうらやましい！）とも言える。

Actually = 本当は cf. To tell the truth,やThe truth is...でも同じ／**by myself** = 自分だけで／**socialize with ~** = ～と[うまく]付き合う

I want to have lunch by myself, but I have to eat with others to socialize.（一人でランチしたいけど、付き合いで皆と食べなくちゃ）と言ってもよい。

---

digestion = 消化／**talk about work** = 仕事のことを話す cf. talk about businessでもよい／**while eating** = 食べながら、食べているときに

Talking about business while eating will upset your stomach.（食べながら仕事の話をすると胃の調子が悪くなるよ）でも同じ。

---

lunch hour = 昼休み cf. lunch breakも同じ／**a great time to ~** = ～する絶好の機会だ／**exchange information** = 情報交換する

「昼休みにほかの人たちと情報交換をした」と言うなら I exchanged information with others during lunch break.。

---

check out ~ = ～を調べる、確認する／**on the Net** = インターネットで cf. on the Internetでも同じ

「インターネットで最新情報を入手する」なら I get the newest information from/through the Internet.。

chapter 6 Taking a Break

25 あれ、いつも来てたヤクルトレディーはどうしたの?
Hey, what happened to the *Yakult* Lady," who always came here to sell and deliver *Yakult* beverages?

26 今週はお昼の電話当番だ。
It's my turn to watch the phone during lunch hour this week.

27 この資格の勉強のために昼休みを有効活用したい。
I want to use my lunch break effectively to study for this qualification.

28 昼に10分でも寝ておくと、午後の仕事がはかどるのよね。
If I can take a 10-minute nap during lunchtime, then I'll be able to work much better in the afternoon.

29 歯磨きと化粧直しをする人で洗面所はいっぱいだ。
The restroom is crowded with women brushing their teeth and reapplying their makeup.

30 あの子昼休みに全部メイク落として、フルメイクやり直すんだって。
That girl takes off all her makeup and completely reapplies it during lunch break.

what happened to ~? = ~に何があったの?、~はどうした?／**deliver =** 配達する／**beverage =** 飲み物、飲料

「ヤクルトレディー」はそのままでは英語では通じないので説明が必要。always came here（いつも来ていた）の代わりに used to come here（以前よく来ていた）としてもよい。

It's my turn to ~ = 自分が~する番だ cf. turn = 順番／**watch the phone = 電話番をする**

「電話番をする」は answer the phone calls（電話に出る）、または handle the phone call（電話に応対する）と言うこともできる。

---

use ~ to ... = ~を…のために使う／**effectively =** 有効に、効率よく／**study for ~ =** ~のための勉強をする／**qualification =** 資格

ほかに I want to use my lunch hour in the most effective way possible to study for this qualification. や I want to get the most out of my lunch break by studying for this qualification. と言い換えられる。

---

take a nap = 昼寝する／**10-minute =** 10分間の／ **work much better =** 仕事がずっとよくできる

「能率が悪くなったら（ペースについていけなくなったら）、やめて休みなさい」は You should stop and rest if you can't keep up the pace. と言う。

---

restroom = 化粧室、洗面所 cf. 洗面台 = wash stand、washbasin／**be crowded with ~ =** ~で混雑している／**brush one's teeth =** 歯を磨く／**reapply one's makeup =** 化粧直しをする cf. makeup = 化粧

前半は「洗面所は女性でいっぱいだ」The restroom is <u>full of</u> / <u>filled with</u> women と言ってもよい。

---

take off one's makeup = 化粧を落とす cf. remove one's makeup でも同じ／**completely =** 完全に／**reapply =** 再びつける

「化粧をする」は <u>wear</u> / <u>put on</u> makeup、「化粧品」は cosmetics。「お化粧を直さなくちゃ」は I need to fix up my makeup. と言う。

chapter 6 Taking a Break

31 昼休みのうちに公共料金の振込をすませとこう。
I should pay the utility bills during this lunch hour.

32 お昼時の郵便局はすごい行列だ。
The line at the post office is so long at lunchtime.

33 クレイン社からの頂き物のお菓子でーす。経理部の皆さんでどうぞ。
Here are some sweets from Crane company! Could you pass them around to everyone in the accounting department?

34 同僚がアイスを差し入れてくれた。
My colleague brought some ice cream to pass around [in the office].

35 脳が疲れたときは、やっぱりチョコレートだね。
When I feel like my brain is tired, chocolate is the one thing that works.

36 最近、仕事中に間食し過ぎかも。
These days I'm snacking too much during work.

utility bill = 公共料金、水道光熱費 cf. utility = 役に立つもの、[電気・ガス・水道などの]公共施設 | bill = 請求書

「銀行振り込みで支払う」なら pay through a bank transfer、「オンラインでの振り込み」なら online transfer over the Internet となる。

---

line = 列／**post office =** 郵便局／**so long =** とても長い cf. very long でも同じ

「郵便局で長い列に並ぶ」なら I stand in a long line at the post office.、「長蛇の列を作る」は make a long line。

Here are ~ = ここに~がある／**sweets =** お菓子、甘いもの／**pass ~ around =** ~を配る／**accounting department =** 経理部

「頂き物」は直訳すると gift だが、sweets from Crane company だけで「頂き物」のニュアンスが出るので訳出する必要はない。

---

colleague = 同僚／**brought =** 持ってきた（**bring** の過去・過去分詞形）／**ice cream =** アイスクリーム

「差し入れ」は「~を[人のために]持ってくる」と表現できる。「サンドイッチの差し入れを持ってきたよ」なら I brought you some sandwiches. と言う。

---

feel like ~ = ~のような気がする／**brain =** 脳、頭脳／**work =** 効く、効き目がある、役に立つ

前半は When I get tired and my brain is not working properly（疲れて脳がちゃんと働かないときに）と言い換えられる。

---

these days = この頃、近頃 cf. lately または recently でも同じ／**snack =** 間食する cf. 名詞で「間食、おやつ」／**during work =** 仕事中に cf. while working でも同じ

「間食をやめる」は stop snacking/eating between meals。

chapter 6 Taking a Break

37 彼女に話してしまうと、次の日には会社中に知れわたってるよ。

If you tell her something, then the next day it'll be all over the office.

38 彼女たち、社内ゴシップをあんな大きな声で。全部筒抜けだって教えてあげるべき？

These girls are gossiping so loudly. Should I tell them that we can hear everything they are talking about?

the next day = 翌日、その次の日／**all over the office** = 会社中で cf. all over the place = あらゆる所に、至る所で

If you tell her your secret, then the next day everyone in the office will know about it.（彼女に秘密を教えたら、翌日には会社中の人が知っているよ）と言い換えられる。

---

gossip = うわさ話をする cf. 名詞で「ゴシップ、うわさ話」／**loudly** = 大声で cf. in such big voicesでも同じ。「小声で」はquietly、in low voices／**Should I ~?** = ～した方がいいだろうか

「彼は黙っていることができない、おしゃべりだ」は He can't keep his mouth shut.、「おしゃべりな（口が軽い）人」は big mouth。

Skit 休憩編

一食入魂！ 給料日のランチはどこで食べる？

Woman： It's payday, so let's have something special for lunch.
Man： I'm going to have my lunch delivered. It's my turn to watch the phone during lunch this week.
W： Actually[1], I should pay my utility bills, but the line at the post office is so long at lunchtime. If I stand in line there, my lunch hour will be over.
M： Why don't you[2] have some soba? That's quick[3].
W： But it's dreary to eat *soba* at a stand-up counter.
M： Every shop is so crowded you might not even get to eat lunch.
W： I could shift my lunch hour to avoid the crowds but I don't like to eat alone.
M： If you wait till one o'clock, I can go with you.
W： Really? That would be great![4]

女性：今日はお給料日だから、ランチは奮発しましょうよ。
男性：僕は出前を頼もうと思って。今週は電話当番だから。
女：ほんとは、私も公共料金の振込しなくちゃいけないんだけど、昼休みの郵便局の行列はものすごく長いから。あの列に並んでたら、お昼休みが終わっちゃうわ。
男：そばにすればいいんじゃない？　それなら早くすむよ。
女：立ち食いそばなんてわびしいわよ。
男：どこも混んでるから、ランチ難民になっちゃうよ。
女：混むのを避けて時間差でお昼に行くこともできるけど、でも一人では食べたくないしね。
男：1時まで待ってくれたら、僕も一緒に行くよ。
女：ほんと？　助かるわ！

【語注】

❶ actually: 実際は、実のところ
❷ Why don't you ~?: 〜したらどうですか
❸ quick: 迅速な、素早い
❹ That would be great!: 嬉しい!、助かる!、素晴らしい!

Quick Check

本章に出てきたフレーズを復習しましょう。以下の日本語の意味になるよう
英文を完成させてください。答えはページの下にあります。

❶散歩して息抜きする。 ➡P159
I ( ) a walk ( ) ( ) ( ).

❷昼休みに用事をすませる。 ➡P160
I ( ) my ( ) ( ) during my lunch break.

❸歯磨きと化粧直しをする。 ➡P161
I ( ) my teeth and ( ) ( ) my ( ).

❹3時のおやつを配る。 ➡P161
I ( ) ( ) ( ) ( ).

❺たまには息抜きしてください。 ➡P162
You ( ) a break ( ) ( ) ( ) ( ).

❻雲隠れしたと思ったら、彼女トイレで眠ってたわ。 ➡P162
She suddenly ( ), ( ) a ( ) in the restroom.

❼最近は煙草を吸える場所を見つけるのにも一苦労だ。 ➡P162
Nowadays I ( ) ( ) finding places where smoking is not ( ).

❽いつもの店は飽きたから、今日は別の店に行こうかな。 ➡P164
I'm rather ( ) ( ) the usual restaurant, so I may ( ) a different one today.

❾あれ、いつも来てたヤクルトレディーはどうしたの？ ➡P170
Hey, ( ) ( ) ( ) the "*Yakult* Lady," who always came here to sell and deliver *Yakult* beverages?

❿彼女に話してしまうと、次の日には会社中に知れわたってるよ。 ➡P174
If you tell her something, then the next day it'll ( ) ( ) ( ) the office.

---

❶take/for/a change ❷get/errands/done ❸brush/freshen/up/makeup ❹pass/out/afternoon/snacks ❺deserve/from/time/to/time ❻disappeared/taking/nap ❼have/trouble/prohibited ❽tired/of/try ❾what/happened/to ❿be/all/over

chapter 7
会議
Meetings

重要事項が決定される場だったり
あるいは単なる時間の無駄だったり。
会議ではさまざまな応酬が
繰り広げられますが、ここでは建前的な
発言より、会議中に心に浮かぶ
「本音」表現に焦点を当てました。

chapter 7 Meetings

Words 単語編

❶会議
❷会合、カジュアルな集まり
❸[定期的な]会議
❹会議、大会、集会
❺討議
❻交渉
❼議長
❽進行役
❾議事日程、議題
❿議題
⓫議事録
⓬出席者
⓭水差し

❶meeting ❷get-together ❸conference ❹convention
❺discussion ❻negotiation ❼chairperson ❽facilitator
❾agenda ❿subject ⓫minutes ⓬attendee ⓭jug ⓮meeting

まずは、さまざまな物や事の名前で
「会議」のシーンのイメージをつかもう。

⑮ホワイトボード
⑯マーカー
⑰プロジェクター
⑱スクリーン
⑲指示棒
⑳レーザーポインター
㉑発表する人
㉒配布資料
㉓プレゼン資料
㉔参考資料
㉕建設的な意見
⑭会議室

⑭room ⑮whiteboard ⑯marker ⑰projector ⑱screen ⑲pointer rod ⑳laser pointer ㉑presenter ㉒handout ㉓presentation material ㉔reference material ㉕constructive suggestion

chapter 7 Meetings

1 会議を設定する
I arrange a meeting.

2 出席人数を確認する
I count the number of attendees.

3 会議の日程を関係者にアナウンスする
I notify the people concerned of the meeting schedule.

4 確認メールを送る
I send an e-mail reminder.

5 前回のペンディング事項を確認する
I find out what was left open during the last meeting.

tips

❷「出席を取る」は、do a roll call または take attendance と言う。
❸ Eメールの冒頭の「関係者各位」は To whom it may concern.。
❹ remind ~ of ... で「~に…を思い出させる」。e.g. The e-mail reminded me of the meeting.(そのEメールで会議のことを思い出した)

6 アジェンダを事前に送付する
I send an agenda in advance to the people concerned.

7 席順を決める
I create a seating arrangement.

8 機材をそろえておく
I have all the equipment ready beforehand.

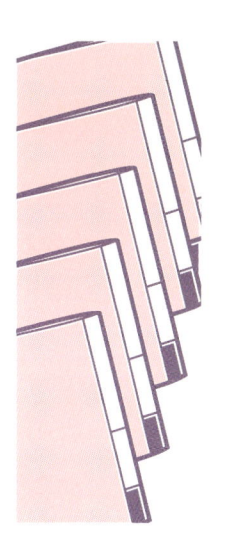

9 会議資料を人数分用意する
I prepare the required number of handouts for the meeting.

10 資料の見せ方に工夫を凝らす
I put a lot of thought into the arrangement of the materials.

❺「ペンディング事項、懸案」はpending matterでもよい。
❻in advanceは「事前に」。❽のbeforehand(前もって)も同意。
❾hand out ~で「~を手渡す」。「会議で資料を[回して]配る」はI pass out handouts in the meeting.。
❿put a lot of thought into ~で「~についてじっくり考える」。

chapter 7 Meetings

11 事前に資料を読み込む
I read up on the material beforehand.

12 根回しをする
I lay the/some groundwork.

13 TV会議の手配をする
I arrange a video teleconference.

14 議長を務める
I chair a meeting.

15 議論を仕切る
I lead/facilitate a discussion.

tips

⓫ read up on ~ で「~を読み込む、予習しておく」。
⓬「根回しをする」は obtain agreement with ~ in advance（事前に~から同意を得ておく）と説明できる。
⓭「~とTV会議をする」は teleconference with ~。
⓯ ミーティングの進行役を facilitator と言う。

16 発言を促す
I prompt someone to speak out.

17 発言するよう指名する
I call on someone to offer a comment.

18 発言を遮る
I cut someone off.

19 議論の方向を修正する
I bring the discussion back on track.

20 意見を調整する
I try to coordinate different views.

⓱ give ~ the floorで「~に発言の場(機会)を与える」。
⓲「~[の発言]を無視する」はpass ~ over。e.g. The facilitator passed her over and kept talking.(進行役は彼女の発言を無視して話し続けた)
⓳ You're getting off the subject.で「[話が]横道にそれているよ」。

chapter 7 Meetings

21 企画の概要を説明する
I give an outline explanation of the plan.

22 アイデアを出し合う
We all pitch in ideas.

23 時計回りにプレゼンをする
We make presentations going around clockwise.

24 質疑応答に入る
We begin a question-and-answer session.

25 意見を交わす
We exchange opinions.

tips

㉑ give a brief overview of the plan でもよい。
㉒「お金を出し合う」は chip in。 e.g. Why don't we all chip in and buy a coffee maker?（みんなでカンパしてコーヒーメーカーを買おう）
㉓「時計と反対回りに」は counterclockwise。
㉔ 質疑応答で「〜からの質問を受け付ける」は take questions from 〜。

26 問題点を指摘する
I point out a problem.

27 反対意見を述べる
I give an opposing opinion.

28 折衷案で合意する
We reach a compromise.

29 妥協案を探る
We seek a compromise.

30 議事録を取る
I take the minutes.

e.g. Now I'm going to take a few questions from the audience.（ここで聴衆の皆様からの質問を承ります）
㉗「賛成意見」は favorable opinion。
㉙ Let's meet each other halfway, here. で「お互いこの辺で妥協し合いましょう」。

chapter 7 Meetings

31 メモを取る
I take notes.

32 あくびをかみ殺す
I try hard not to yawn.

33 内職をする
I work on some other stuff during a meeting.

tips

㉛「メモ」はnote[s]。英語のmemoは「社内回覧文書」(= memorandum) の意味で使うことが多い。
㉜「まばたきして眠気をさます」はblink back sleepと言う。I act like I'm listening.で「聞いているふりをする」。
㉞「10分間[コーヒー／トイレ]休憩を取る」はhave a 10-minute

CD 2
06

34 休憩をはさむ
We pause for a break.

35 会議を再開する
We resume the meeting.

36 多数決を取る
We take a vote.

[coffee/bathroom] break。
㉟ Let's continue where we left off. で「先ほどの続きから始めましょう」。
㊱ vote for(against) ~で「~に賛成(反対)票を投じる」。

chapter 7 Meetings

1. なんでいつもなかなか人がそろわないんだろ？
How come everyone always takes so long to get together for the meeting?

2. 会議の目的を、まずはみんなでしっかり共有しなきゃ。
First of all, we each have to share the common objective of the meeting.

3. 資料はいきわたったかな？
Everyone's got a handout now?

4. うーん、そのプレゼン資料ではアピール度が低いな。
Umm ... I'm afraid the presentation material won't make much of an impression.

5. 資料やデータの準備もせずに会議に出るなんて、彼、使えないな！
He's so useless! Who shows up for a meeting without any reference materials or data?

6. パワポや資料の見やすさも、プレゼンの結果に影響するよね。
The result of your presentation depends also on the viewability of your PowerPoint or material, I think.

How come S + V? = どうして〜なんだろう／get together = 集まる

get-together で「会合、カジュアルな集まり」の意味になる。e.g. We're having a get-together to welcome Mr. Newman on Friday.（金曜日にニューマンさんの歓迎会を行います）

---

first of all = まずはじめに／common objective = 共通の目的

「共通認識」は common understanding/awareness。e.g. The director affirmed the common awareness of the project.（部長はプロジェクトの共通認識を確認した）

---

handout = 配布資料、プリント

handout は「[会議・講座などで配る] 配布資料」のこと。「資料あまっていますか」は Do you have some extra handouts / extras?、「配布資料が足りないみたいだ」は I'm afraid I don't have enough handouts. と言う。

I'm afraid 〜 = 残念だけど〜です／presentation material = プレゼン資料

not make much of 〜 は「大して〜にならない」という意味。e.g. It won't make much of a difference to our workload.（仕事量に関しては大した違いにならないよ）

---

useless = 使えない、無能な／show up for 〜 = 〜に現れる／reference material = 参考資料

「使えない奴、役立たず」は be good for nothing でもよい。e.g. Forgot everything discussed in the meeting? You're good for nothing!（会議で話し合った内容をすべて忘れたって？　この役立たず！）

---

depend on 〜 = 〜に依存する／viewability = 見やすさ

形容詞の viewable は「見ることができる、見やすい」という意味。類義語に easy-to-read（読みやすい）、eye-friendly（目に優しい）がある。e.g. The monitor is eye-friendly.（このスクリーンは目に優しい）

chapter 7 Meetings

7 数字を読み上げるだけじゃ、会議の意味ない。時間の無駄だよ。
Reading out all those figures in a meeting is pointless. It's a waste of time.

---

8 プレゼンはつかみが肝心。
The main thing in a good presentation is having a good hook.

---

9 彼の話し方、声張ってるし滑舌よくて聞きやすい。
He's easy to listen to because he speaks with a loud voice and clear enunciation.

---

10 彼の発言は、いつも理路整然として要点をきっちり押さえてるね。
His speeches are always clear-cut and to the point.

---

11 なるほど、そういう考え方があったか。
I see. Now I'm looking at it in a different way.

---

12 さっきから彼ばっかりしゃべっているな。
He's been the only guy speaking up for a while, hasn't he?

read out ~ = ～を朗読する／pointless = 無意味な／waste of time = 時間の無駄

pointless の point は「要点、意味」。e.g. The point is you should give your opinion.（要するにきみは自分自身の意見を述べるべきだよ）

---

the main thing = 重要なこと／hook = 引きつけるもの、つかみ

hook は本来「フック、留め金」の意味。hook を使った表現には、let ~ off the hook（～を責任から解放する）がある。e.g. My supervisor let me off the hook with a mild reprimand.（上司は軽い叱責だけで見逃してくれた）

---

with a loud voice = 大声で／enunciation = 明瞭に話すこと

「よく通る声」は carrying voice と言う。carry は「[声・音が]届く、伝わる」の意味。e.g. The presenter spoke in a carrying voice so I felt comfortable listening to her.（発表者はよく通る声で話したので、聞いていて心地よかった）

---

clear-cut = 明確な、わかりやすい／to the point = 要領を得た

反対に「的外れの」は off the point。e.g. His argument tends to be off the point.（彼の議論は的外れになりがちです）、To drift off the point, I'm going to transfer to the Osaka branch next month.（余談ですが、来月大阪支社に転勤になります）

---

in a different way = 別の方法で、違った感じで

「目からウロコが落ちた」は The scales fell from my eyes. と言う。scale は「ウロコ」。「斬新な考え方をする」は think outside the box。e.g. Let's think outside the box and come up with a better plan.（考え方を180度変えて、よりよい企画を考え出そう）

---

speak up = 発言する／for a while = しばらくの間

「休まずに話し続ける」は talk nonstop でよい。e.g. She talked nonstop for 30 minutes.（彼女は30分間休まず話し続けた）。また、The greatest talkers are the least doers.（口数の多い人ほど行動が伴わない）ということわざもある。

chapter 7 Meetings

13 君の説明の主旨が伝わってこない。
I really don't get what you're saying here.

14 ちゃんと考えをまとめてから発言して。
Why don't you engage your brain before speaking?

15 結局この話、どこに着地するんだろう？
I wonder where this discussion is going to end up.

16 今の発言、空気読めてないなあ。
Hear what he just said? Obviously, he can't even see what's going on.

17 うわ、この発言、議事録に残せないよ。
Wow, I can't put this word down in the minutes.

18 プレゼンの詰めが甘くて、質問攻めにあった。
Because my presentation obviously slacked off towards the end, they really grilled me.

get(= understand) = 理解する

「〜の主旨を理解する」は follow the gist of 〜 。e.g. Apparently, the chief was not following the gist of your speech.（見た感じ、局長はきみの話の主旨を理解していなかったみたい）

Why don't you 〜? = 〜したらどうですか(提案)／engage one's brain = 頭を働かせる

「考えをまとめる」は organize one's thoughts もよく使う。e.g. You should organize your thoughts before writing e-mail.（メールを書く前に自分の考えをまとめた方がいいよ）

---

end up 〜 = 結局〜になる、終わる、着地する

end up 〜 で「〜という状態で終わる」。e.g. The event ended up failing.（そのイベントは不本意な結果に終わった）。また、「中途半端に終わる」は end up in the air と言う。

---

obviously, 〜 = 誰が見ても〜だ

「座をしらけさせる人、空気を読めない人」を wet blanket（濡れた毛布）と言う。e.g. He's such a wet blanket, offering only negative feedback.（否定的な感想しか言わないなんて、彼はなんて空気を読めない奴なんだ）

---

put 〜 down = 〜を書き留める／minutes = 議事録

「〜を書き留める」は write 〜 down、take 〜 down でもよい。「[会議で] 議事録を取る」は take minutes。e.g. I think I need more work on how to take minutes.（議事録の取り方をもっと勉強しないと）。

---

slack off towards the end = 最後で勢いが衰える、詰めが甘い／grill 〜 = 〜を質問攻めにする

slack off は「怠ける」の意味でもよく使う。e.g. Don't slack off.（手を抜くな）。grill（グリル＜直火＞で焼く）は会話で「矢継ぎ早に質問する」という意味で使われる動詞。

chapter 7 Meetings

19 ハッシュさんが進行役だとスムーズに進む。
Meetings always go smoothly when Mr. Hush is the facilitator.

20 スターンさんが会議に参加すると引き締まる。
With Mr. Stern in a meeting, everyone sits bolt upright.

21 部長の話、すぐ脱線する。
The manager gets sidetracked so often.

22 もっと建設的な意見を言ってよ。
Couldn't you come up with some more constructive suggestions?

23 この前の案の焼き直しじゃないか。
Hey, this is a total rehash of the previous plan.

24 前回の打ち合わせから何も進展していない。
Nothing on this matter has made progress since the last meeting.

facilitator = 進行役

「会議の進行役を務める」は lead the meeting でもよい。facilitate は「〜を容易にする、円滑に進める」という意味。e.g. This software facilitates my work.（このソフトのおかげで仕事がはかどる）

---

with 〜 = 〜がいれば／sit bolt upright = 背筋を伸ばして座る

[bolt] upright は「背筋を伸ばして、まっすぐに」の意味。「場を和ませる」は break the ice。e.g. Ms. Jordan broke the ice with a joke.（ジョーダンさんがジョークで場を和ませた）

---

get sidetracked = [話が]横道にそれる、脱線する

「脱線する」は、stray off the subject（本題から外れる）でもよい。track は「[話の] 筋」。on the [right] track で「本題に沿った」。e.g. Am I on the right track?（ずれた話をしていないですよね）、Let's get the discussion back on the track.（議論を元に戻しましょう）

Couldn't you 〜? = 〜できないのかな／come up with 〜 = 〜を考えつく／constructive = 建設的な

この文脈では constructive は practical（実践的な）、helpful（役立つ）、productive（生産的な）と言い換えることができる。

Hey = おいおい／rehash = 焼き直し／previous = 以前の

「書き直し[する]」は rewrite。e.g. The proposal is very much the same as the earlier one, so please rewrite it.（以前の企画書とほとんど同じなので、書き直してください）

---

make progress = 進展する／since 〜 = 〜からずっと

progress は「進捗状況」の意味でもよく使われる。e.g. I have to report the progress of the project to my boss.（プロジェクトの進捗状況を上司に報告しないと）

chapter 7 Meetings

25 現場の意見が全く取り入れられないんだ。
Managers never listen to the staff working under them.

26 いつだって声の大きい人の意見が通るんだよな。
The squeaky wheel always seems to win in discussions.

27 それって机上の空論じゃないの?
That's a bit pie in the sky, isn't it?

28 数字的な裏付けがないと説得力に欠けるよ。
Your explanation won't be persuasive without numerical evidence.

29 みんな興奮して大声で次から次へと話すから、眠気も吹っ飛んだ。
Everyone got excited as hell and just started speaking one after another, which really shook off my sleepiness.

30 どちらの言い分もそれぞれわかるんだけど、やっぱり……。
I appreciate both sides of the situation, but still …

manager = 管理職／listen to ~ = [意見]に耳を傾ける

「一般社員、平社員」は<u>rank-and-file employee</u> / <u>rank-and-filer</u> と言う。e.g. The management usually doesn't think highly of the views of the rank-and-filers.（この会社＜経営陣＞は基本的に平社員の意見を尊重しない）

---

squeaky wheel = 声の大きい人、ごねる人

squeaky wheel の文字通りの意味は「キーキー鳴る車輪」。The squeaky wheel gets the grease.（きしる車輪は油を差してもらえる：主張する人は求めるものを与えられる）という意味のイディオムがある。

---

pie in the sky = 絵に描いた餅、机上の空論

「机上の空論」は <u>desk/armchair</u> plan でも OK。ほかに pie を使ったイディオムとしては It's easy as pie.（朝飯前だよ）、I have my fingers in two pies.（二足のわらじを履いている）などがある。

---

explanation = 説明／persuasive = 説得力のある／numerical evidence = 数字的証拠

「説得力のある説明」は convincing explanation。逆に「説得力のない説明」は lame explanation と言う。e.g. That's a lame explanation. I don't buy it.（ヘタな説明だね。それじゃ信じられないよ）

---

as hell = ものすごく（かなりくだけた言い方）／one after another = 次々に／shook off ~ = ~を振り払った（shookはshakeの過去形）

as hell は「ものすごく」という意味。e.g. I'm as hungry as hell.（ものすごくお腹がすいている）。Shake it off!（それを振り払え）は「気にするな！」という意味でよく使われる掛け声。

---

appreciate ~ = ~を十分に理解する

hear both sides で「両方の意見を聞く」。「~に関して言い分がある」は have a say in ~ と言う。e.g. I have a say in this matter.（この件について申し上げたいことがあります）

chapter 7 Meetings

31 早く本題に入ってください。
Cut to the chase, please.

---

32 人の話の腰を折らないでよ。
Let me finish, will you?

---

33 何だかこっちの旗色が悪くなってきたぞ。
I don't know why, but the odds seem against us now.

---

34 よし、目論んでいた通りに話が進んだ。
Good! The discussion proceeded as planned.

---

35 堂々巡りだ。いったん仕切り直した方がいい。
The discussion is going in circles. We should stop now and make a fresh start later.

---

36 そろそろまとめに入ろうか。
Why don't we wrap it up now?

cut to the chase = ずばり要点を言う

類似表現に get down to brass tacks（話の核心に移る）がある。逆に「遠回しな言い方をする」は beat around the bush。e.g. Stop beating around the bush and tell me how you really feel.（遠回しな言い方はやめて、本当に思っていることを教えて）

---

will you? = 〜してください（命令文の最後に付く）

Let me finish. で「私の話を最後まで聞いてください」。「人の話をさえぎる、腰を折る」は cut ~ off。e.g. I cut her off and changed the topic.（彼女の話をさえぎって話題を変えた）

---

odds = 勝つ見込み、旗色

odds are against ~ で「〜には分が悪い」。against all odds（大きな困難にもかかわらず）という表現もある。「形勢、潮目」は tide とも言う。e.g. The tide seems to be turning.（形勢が変わってきたみたいだ）

Good! = よし！／proceed = 進行する／as ~ = 〜のように

「計画通りに行く」は turn out as planned でもよい。「よく練られた計画」は best-laid plan と言う。e.g. The best-laid plans go astray.（イディオム：物事はなかなか計画通りにはいかない）

---

go in circles = 堂々巡りする／make a fresh start = 新たに踏み出す、再出発する

「振り出しに戻る」は go back to square one。e.g. I think we should go back to square one and start from scratch.（最初に戻ってゼロからやり直した方がよいと思います）

Why don't we ~ ? = 〜しましょうか（提案）／wrap ~ up = 〜を切り上げる

It's about time ~（そろそろ〜の時間だ）を使って It's about time we were wrapping it up. と言うこともできる。「今日はこれで終わりにしよう、切り上げよう」は Let's call it a day. と言う。

chapter 7 Meetings

37 多数決なら完全にこちらが有利だ。
Taking a vote will definitely give us an edge.

38 また結論先送りか。
The decision has been put on the back burner again.

39 結局、上司の鶴の一声で決着がついた。
As it turned out, what put an end to the discussion was a word from the boss.

40 議論が白熱して、会議が長引いたね。
The debate heated up, so the meeting dragged on and on.

take a vote = 票決する／**definitely** = 間違いなく／**give ~ an edge** = ~を有利にする

「挙手によって票決する」は vote by a show of hands。e.g. We had a vote by a show of hands at the end of the meeting.（会議の最後に挙手による採決を取った）

---

put ~ on the back burner = ~を後回しにする

put ~ on the back burner の文字通りの意味は「~を後列のレンジに置く」。問題の解決や決定を「棚上げする」は日本語と同じく put ~ on the shelf と言う。e.g. The remodeling project has been put on the shelf.（改装計画は棚上げになった）

---

as it turned out = 結果的に／**what** = ~したもの（先行詞を含む関係代名詞）／**put an end to ~** = ~を終わらせる／**word** = 一言、発言

「~が一件落着する」は be settled。e.g. The matter was settled with a compromise.（その件は妥協案によって一件落着した）

---

heat up = 白熱する、ヒートアップする／**drag on and on** = 長引く

「長引く」は take forever（いつまでも続く）を使っても表現できる。e.g. The monthly meeting seemed to take forever.（月例会議は永遠に終わらないかに思えた）

「起き寝る」流・ビジネス英語 その❸

ビジネスシーンでの効果的なプレゼンの仕方

1. プレゼンの流れと表現例

プレゼン（presentation）には大まかな流れがあり、ある程度決まった表現が使われることが多い。以下(1)～(5)で流れと英語の表現例を挙げておく。

1. 挨拶、話し手の紹介
<u>Good morning, everyone.</u>/<u>Good afternoon, ladies and gentlemen.</u> My name is …. （皆様、おはようございます／こんにちは。…と申します）

2. プレゼンの主要な目的と全体の構成
Today, I'd like to talk about … /The purpose of my talk today is … （本日は…について話をさせていただきたく思います／本日の話の目的は…です）
I have divided my talk into three parts./I'm going to talk about three areas.（話を3つの部分に分けました／3つの分野に関して話をします）

3. 具体的な個々のポイントの説明、資料、根拠など
First,… （最初に、…）
Next,…/Second,… （次に、…／2番目に、…）
Finally,… （最後に、…）

4. まとめ
I'd like to summarize my main points again. （主要なポイントをもう一度まとめたいと思います）
Thank you for <u>your attention</u>/<u>listening</u>. （ご清聴ありがとうございました）

5. 質疑応答
If there are any questions, I'll be glad to answer them. （ご質問があれば喜んでお答えいたします）

荒井 貴和　Text by Kiwa Arai

2. プレゼンの構成の立て方、話し方

　構成としては、最初にプレゼンの目的は何なのかをはっきりさせてから具体的なポイントに入るのが基本である。**大切なのは「結論から述べる」**こと。最も言いたいことを言ってから、具体的に説明したり、裏付けなどを述べるようにしよう。**個々のポイントを述べた後で、プレゼンの最後に締めくくり**としてもう一度主要なポイントをまとめて述べるとよい。大切なポイントが何だったのかを聞き手に印象づけてプレゼンを終わらせるようにしたい。なお、プレゼンでは**フォーマルな表現が基本**となるので、くだけた表現を使ったり、カジュアルな口調になったりしないように注意しよう。

　プレゼンでは、はっきりと明確に話すことが大前提となる。自分の英語や話す内容に自信がないと声が小さくかつ早口になりがちだが、わかりにくくなるだけだ。**落ち着いた口調で少しゆっくり話した方が聞きやすい**。また、**ボディランゲージ**（体の動き、姿勢、顔の表情など）も重要である。自分のメモ（原稿）やスライドばかり見るのではなく、**必ず聞き手を見ながら**（アイコンタクトをとりながら）話すようにしよう。

　なお、「私は英語が下手なので、わかりにくいかもしれません」といった言い訳は不要なだけでなく、自分のプレゼンに対して不利な先入観を与えるだけなので、たとえ謙遜であっても言わないようにすべきである。

　効果的なプレゼンのためには、**視覚に訴える資料やパワーポイントのスライドなどを活用**して、伝えたい要点をはっきりさせるとよい。パワーポイントの場合、1枚のスライドに情報を盛り込みすぎないように気をつけよう。プレゼンを聞くよりも、スライドの文字や情報を読む方が中心になっては本末転倒だ。スライドや資料はあくまでプレゼンの補助と考えて、必要な情報をできるだけシンプルかつ効果的に提示しよう。

　忘れてはならないのが、与えられた**時間内にプレゼンを終了**させることである。質疑応答の時間の余裕をとって終えられるように時間配分を考えて、十分に準備・リハーサルをしてからプレゼンに臨もう。

Skit 会議編

ジャックは理想の会議進行役

Woman: Good! The discussion proceeded as planned. Today's meeting went really well[1].

Man: Meetings always go smoothly when Jack is the facilitator.

W: Yes, he lays the groundwork and his speeches are always clear-cut and to the point.

M: The manager gets side-tracked so often, but Jack brings the discussion back on track.

W: I like how we all pitch in ideas and exchange opinions so we can coordinate different views.

M: But it's also important to know when to pause for a break and then resume the meeting.

W: Yes, Jack really knows how to chair a meeting.

M: I think we should take him out for a drink[2]. What do you say?[3]

女性：よかった、思いどおりに話が進んで。今日の会議は本当にうまくいったわ。
男性：ジャックが進行役だと、会議がスムースに運ぶね。
女：そうなの、根回しもちゃんとするし、発言はいつも理路整然として要点をきっちり押さえているし。
男：部長の話はすぐ脱線するけど、ジャックは議論の方向を修正してくれるしな。
女：私、みんなでアイデアを出し合って、意見を交わしながら、いろいろな意見を調整していくその過程が好きなのよねえ。
男：あと、休憩をはさみながら会議を再開させていくタイミングを測るのも重要だよね。
女：そう、ジャックは本当に会議の仕切り方を心得ているわ。
男：今度彼を飲みに誘ったらどうかな。どう思う？

【語 注】

❶ go well: うまくいく　　う）
❷ take ~ out for a drink: ~を飲み会に連れ出す
❸ What do you say?: どう？　どう思う？（誘ったり、意見を聞いたりするときに使

Quick Check

本章に出てきたフレーズを復習しましょう。以下の日本語の意味になるよう
英文を完成させてください。答えはページの下にあります。

❶前回のペンディング事項を確認する。 ➡P182
I find out what was ( ) ( ) during the last meeting.

❷資料の見せ方に工夫を凝らす。 ➡P183
I ( ) ( ) ( ) ( ) ( ) into the arrangement of the materials.

❸プレゼンはつかみが肝心。 ➡P192
The main thing in a good presentation is having a ( ) ( ).

❹いつだって声の大きい人の意見が通るんだよな。 ➡P198
The ( ) ( ) always seems to ( ) in discussions.

❺それって机上の空論じゃないの? ➡P198
That's a bit ( ) ( ) ( ) ( ), isn't it?

❻早く本題に入ってください。 ➡P200
( ) ( ) ( ) ( ), please.

❼何だかこっちの旗色が悪くなってきたぞ。 ➡P200
I don't know ( ), but the ( ) seem ( ) ( ) now.

❽そろそろまとめに入ろうか。 ➡P200
( ) don't we ( ) it ( ) now?

❾多数決なら完全にこちらが有利だ。 ➡P202
( ) ( ) ( ) will definitely ( ) us ( ) ( ).

❿また結論先送りか。 ➡P202
The decision has been ( ) ( ) ( ) ( ) ( ) again.

---

❶left/open ❷put/a/lot/of/thought ❸good/hook ❹squeaky/wheel/win ❺pie/in/the/sky ❻Cut/to/the/chase ❼why/odds/against/us ❽Why/wrap/up ❾Taking/a/vote/give/an/edge ❿put/on/the/back/burner

chapter 8
社内行事
Company Events

以前ほどではないにせよ、「朝礼」
「花見」「忘年会」などなど、
社内行事が恒例化している会社は、
まだまだ多いのではないでしょうか。
ここでは「一本締め」「無礼講」など、
日本特有の表現も紹介しています。

chapter 8 Company Events

Words 単語編

❶朝礼 ❷演壇
❸年頭の挨拶
❹記念式典
❺社歌
❻送別会
❼歓迎会
❽忘年会
❾花見
❿乾杯
⓫宴会芸、隠し芸

❶morning staff meeting ❷podium ❸New Year's speech
❹anniversary ceremony ❺company song ❻farewell party
❼welcome party ❽end-of-the-year party ❾cherry-blossom-viewing party ❿toast ⓫party trick ⓬inter-division bowling

CD2 09

まずは、さまざまな物や事の名前で
「社内行事」のシーンのイメージをつかもう。

⑬ボーリング場

⑮ゴルフコンペ
⑯社内運動会
⑰社内旅行
⑱研修
⑲健康診断
⑳大掃除

㉑祝電
㉒祝辞
㉓ご祝儀

⑫部署対抗
　ボーリング大会

⑭チームワーク

tournament　⑬bowling alley　⑭teamwork　⑮golf competition
⑯company sports day　⑰company trip　⑱on-the-job-training
⑲physical checkup　⑳year-end cleaning　㉑congratulatory telegram　㉒congratulatory speech　㉓gift money

chapter 8 Company Events

1 朝礼に出る
I attend a morning staff meeting.

2 親睦会の手配をする
I arrange/organize a get-acquainted meeting.

3 乾杯の音頭をとる(乾杯する)
I propose(make) a toast.

4 送別会の幹事になる
I take charge of the farewell party.

5 歓迎会のお店を予約する
I reserve a restaurant for the welcome party.

tips

❷ get acquainted で「知り合いになる、懇意になる」。
❸ toast は「乾杯、乾杯の挨拶」、また動詞で「乾杯する」。
❹ farewell は「別れ[の]」、take charge of ~ は「~の世話をする」で、ここでは代わりに organize（計画して開催する）を使ってもよい。
❺ reserve は「~を予約する」、make a reservation [at ~] でも同じ。

6 ネットで送別会用の店を探す
On the Internet, I look for a restaurant for the farewell party.

7 部長にビールをお酌する
I pour the [division] manager a beer.

8 忘年会の司会をする
I M.C. the end-of-the-year party.

9 花見に参加する
I go to a cherry-blossom-viewing party.

10 ゴルフの社内コンペに出る
I enter the company golf competition.

❼ I pour a beer for the manager. と言ってもよい。
❽ M.C. は元々 master of ceremonies（司会者）の略で、「司会をする」という動詞になった。「忘年会」は year-end party でも。
❿ enter は「加わる、出場する」。「コンペ」は competition（競技会、コンテスト）を省略した和製英語。

chapter 8 Company Events

11 研修を受ける
I get on-the-job training.

12 会社の健康診断を受ける
I have a physical checkup arranged by the company.

13 同僚の結婚式に出る
I attend my colleague's wedding reception.

14 同僚の結婚祝いのカンパをする
I pitch in some money for my co-worker's wedding gift.

tips

⓫ on-the-job は「実地の、実際に仕事をしながら習得する」。
⓬「健康診断」は medical checkup、また単に checkup とも。「健康診断のため医者に行く」は go see a doctor for a checkup。
⓮「カンパする」は <u>contribute</u> / <u>chip in</u> some money でもよい。
⓯ congratulatory は「祝いの」。「祝う」は congratulate、名詞の複数形で

15 祝電をネットで申し込む
I use the Internet to send a congratulatory telegram.

16 部下の結婚式で祝辞を述べる
I make a congratulatory speech at my staff member's wedding.

17 クライアントの父親が亡くなったので、弔電の手配をする
The client's father has passed away, so I arrange for a condolence telegram [to be sent].

18 香典を包む
I prepare condolence money for the funeral.

Congratulations! なら「おめでとう！」になる。
⓰ make a speech（スピーチをする）は <u>deliver</u>/<u>give</u> a speech でもよい。
⓱ pass away（亡くなる）は die（死ぬ）より婉曲な言い方。condolence は「お悔やみ、哀悼」。

chapter 8 Company Events

1. いつか大口顧客をゲットして表彰されたい。
One day, I'd like to get a big client and receive an award.

2. 社長の話、相変わらずループしてて長いなあ。
The president's speech is repetitive and goes on and on as usual.

3. 今度のプロジェクトが落ち着いたら、部署のみんなでパーッと飲みに行こう。
When this project settles down, let's all go drinking and have some fun!

4. みんなの予定がなかなか合わない。
It's difficult for everyone to agree on the schedule.

5. センター長の隣の席だけはいや！
I just don't want to sit next to the center director!

6. 斎藤さんが部長に絡んでる。無礼講って真に受けちゃだめだよ。
Mr. Saito is picking fights with the boss. He shouldn't take "bureiko" at face value and ignore rank and manners.

one day = いつの日か／**big client** = 大口の顧客／**receive an award** = 賞をもらう cf. award = 賞

「表彰されるのは私の夢だ」は It's my dream to receive an award.。「賞をいただけて、大変光栄です」と言うなら It is a great honor to receive the award.。

---

repetitive = 繰り返しの、くどくどと繰り返す／**go on and on** = 延々と続ける、長々と述べる／**as usual** = いつものように

「スピーチをする」は <u>make</u>/<u>deliver</u>/<u>give</u> a speech、「即席でスピーチをする」なら give a speech on the spot、「簡潔なスピーチ」は <u>short</u>/<u>brief</u> speech。

---

settle down = 落ち着く／**go drinking** = 飲みに行く／**have fun** = 楽しむ

「パーッとやろう、騒ごう！」は Let's go out and party! や Let's party! という言い方もある。

It's difficult for ~ to ... = ～にとって…するのは難しい／**agree on ~** = ～について一致する

「予定が詰まっている」は My schedule is full.、「予定を調整（変更）する」は I <u>adjust</u>(<u>change</u>) my schedule. と言う。

---

just = ただ～だけ／**next to ~** = ～の隣に／**center director** = センター長 cf. director = ［施設などの］所長、～長

I just want to avoid sitting next to the center director!（センター長の隣に座るのだけは避けたい）でも同じ。

---

pick fights with ~ = ～に絡む　cf. be rude to ~ = ～に無礼な態度をとる／**take ~ at face value** = ～をそのまま受け止める、真に受ける cf. at face value = 文字通りの意味で／**ignore** = 無視する

「無礼講」はそのままでは英語では通じないので ignore rank and manners（序列や礼儀を無視する）と補足している。

chapter 8 Company Events

7 彼、普段と飲んだときの差が激しいねえ。
He's totally different once he gets drunk.

8 ラッキー、ビンゴで旅行券が当たった!
Hooray! I won a travel coupon at the bingo game!

9 今までお世話になりました。
Thank you very much for everything [you have done for me].

10 あなたがいなくなると寂しくなるわ。次の職場でも頑張ってね。
I'll miss you when you're gone. I wish you good luck, and keep up the good work at your new workplace.

11 忘年会続きで体がもたないよ。
I don't know if I can survive all these year-end parties.

12 去年の忘年会は酔っ払って大失敗しちゃったから、今年はおとなしくしてよう。
I got totally drunk and screwed up at the last year-end party, so I'll try to lay low [and stay sober] this year.

totally = すっかり、全く／**once ~** = 一度〜すると／**get drunk** = 酔う、酔っぱらう cf. drunk = 酔って

He changes a lot when he gets drunk.（彼は飲むとずいぶん変わってしまう）と言ってもよい。

Hooray! = やったー!、ばんざい! cf. ほかにYes!、All right!など。この場合Lucky!は不適切／**won** = 当たった、獲得した(winの過去・過去分詞形)／**travel coupon** = 旅行券 cf. coupon = 優待券、クーポン

ゲームの「賞品」は prize。「賞品をゲットする」は win a prize。

---

for everything = すべてに対して／**you have done for me** = あなたが私にしてくれた

Thank you for all of your help.（何から何までお世話になりました）と言ってもよい。

---

miss = 〜がいないのを寂しく思う／**wish ~ good luck** = 〜がうまくいくことを願う／**keep up the good work** = 頑張って、よい仕事をしてください cf. keep up = 頑張り続ける／**workplace** = 職場

この場合「頑張る」は「新しい職場でもよい仕事を続ける」ことなので、英語ではこのように具体的に言う必要がある。

I don't know if ~ = 〜かどうかわからない／**survive** = 生き延びる、何とかやっていける／**year-end party** = 忘年会 cf. end-of-the-year partyも同じ

I have so many year-end parties that I don't know if I can make it.（忘年会が多すぎて乗り切れるかどうかわからない）でもよい。

---

get drunk = 酔っぱらう／**screw up** = 大失敗する、しくじる／**lay low** = 鳴りをひそめている、おとなしくする／**stay sober** = 酔わずにいる cf. sober = しらふの

「酔っぱらい」は a drunk、「酔いがさめた」と言うなら I sobered up.。

chapter 8 Company Events

13 忘年会の出し物、今年は何にするかなあ、頭が痛いよ。
What kind of party trick should I do for the year-end party? It's a pain in the neck.

14 斉藤さんっておとなしそうだけど、なかなかの芸人ね。
Mr. Saito seems reserved and very quiet, so I never guessed he'd be so entertaining at a party.

15 彼、仕事もあのくらい張り切ってくれればいいのにねえ。
I wish he would work on his job as enthusiastically as he acts at parties.

16 部長、一本締めお願いします！
Boss, let's wrap up the party with "ipponjime"!

17 今度、部署対抗ボーリング大会を会社が主催するんだって。
I hear the company will hold an inter-division bowling tournament.

18 ボーリング大会の参加は必須でなく任意です。
It's up to you whether you take part in the bowling tournament; it's not obligatory.

what kind of = どういう[種類の]／**party trick** = 宴会芸、隠し芸　cf. trick = 芸当、手技／**a pain in the neck** = 悩みの種 cf. neck = 首

「頭が痛い」は It gives me a headache.（頭痛の種になる）と言うこともできる。

---

reserved = 控えめな／**quiet** = 無口な／**I never guessed ~** = ~とは思いもよらなかった／**he'd be so ~** = とても~になる('d = would)／**entertaining** = 愉快な、面白い cf. entertain = ~を楽しませる

プロの「芸人」は comedian や entertainer だが、ここでは「他人を楽しませる[一般の]人」のことなので、これらの語は使わない。

I wish ~ = ~ならいいのにと思う／**as ~ as ...** = ...と同じくらい~／**enthusiastically** = 熱心に、夢中になって

直訳すると「宴会と同じぐらい仕事を熱心にしてくれればいいのに」となる。

---

wrap up = 締めくくる、まとめる cf. Let's wrap up the party. = パーティーはお開きです

「一本締め」は日本の習慣なので ceremonial clapping of the hands by all at a party（参加者全員で儀礼として手をたたくこと）のような説明が必要。

I hear ~ = ~と聞いている、~だそうですね／**hold** = 開く、開催する／**inter-division** = 部署対抗の cf. inter-~ = ~間の、相互の | division = 課、部／**tournament** = [勝ち抜き]試合、大会

「大会は来週開催されます」なら The tournament will be held next week.。

It's up to you = あなた次第です cf. up to ~ = ~次第で／**whether ~** = ~かどうか／**take part in ~** = ~に参加する／**obligatory** = 強制的な、必須の

「ボーリングに行く」は go bowling、「ボーリング場」は bowling alley。

chapter 8 Company Events

19 ボーリング大会ではチームワークが試される。
We cannot win the bowling tournament without teamwork.

20 ＜ゴルフ場で見事なショットを打った人へ＞ナイスショット！
Great shot!

21 思えば初仕事は、花見の場所取りと買い出しだったなあ。
When I think about it, my first job was finding a good spot for cherry-blossom viewing and getting food and drinks for the party.

22 同僚の結婚式っていくら包めばいいんだろう？
How much money should I give as a gift for my colleague's wedding?

23 結婚式ラッシュで 御祝儀がつらい。
I have to attend <u>a whole bunch of</u>/<u>a lot of</u> wedding receptions, and it's expensive to come up with all that gift money.

24 もうすぐ健康診断か。今年はどこも悪いとこありませんように。
My regular health checkup is coming up. I hope nothing is wrong with me this year.

win the tournament = 大会に勝つ、優勝する／without ~ = ~なしで
英文を直訳すると「チームワークなしでは大会で勝てない」となる。「チームワークが勝利のカギだ」と言うなら Teamwork is the key to victory..

---

great shot は <u>nice</u>/<u>beautiful</u> shot でもよい。ゴルフに限らずプレーヤーに「お見事！」「やったー！」などと声を掛けるときは、<u>Nice!</u> / <u>Yes!</u> / <u>All right!</u> といった表現がよく使われる。

When I think about it = 考えてみると／a good spot for ~ = ~にいい場所／cherry-blossom viewing = 花見 cf. cherry blossom = 桜の花 | cherry-blossom viewing season = お花見の季節
「花見客でにぎわっていた」は There were a lot of people <u>enjoying</u>/<u>coming to see</u> the cherry blossoms. と言う。

---

give ~ as a gift = ~を贈り物にする／wedding = 結婚式、婚礼 cf. wedding present = 結婚祝いの贈り物
欧米では結婚祝いにお金を包むのではなく、あらかじめカップルが欲しい品物のリストをデパートなどに登録（bridal registry）し、そこから予算に合った品物を選んでもらうのが一般的。

---

attend = 出席する／wedding reception = 結婚披露宴／expensive = 高い、金がかかる／come up with ~ = ~を工面する、用意する／gift money = 御祝儀
「結婚式と披露宴に招待された」は I was invited to the wedding ceremony and reception..。「二次会」は <u>after</u>/<u>follow-up</u> party。

---

regular = 定期的な／health checkup = 健康診断 cf.「健康診断」はほかに [<u>physical</u>/<u>medical</u>] checkupなど**／come up = 近づく／nothing is wrong with ~ = ~に全く問題がない、大丈夫**
「定期的に健康診断を受けている」は I have a <u>health</u>/<u>physical</u> checkup regularly..

chapter 8 Company Events

25 メタボで引っ掛からないか、ウエストが気になるなあ。
I'm worried about my waistline. Does it exceed the standard for <u>being overweight</u>/<u>obesity</u>?

26 ガーン、また視力が落ちてるよ。
<u>Oh, no!</u>/<u>What a shock!</u> My eyesight got worse again!

27 去年と数値が変わってなくて安心した。
I'm relieved that the results of the medical checkup haven't changed from last year.

be worried about ~ = ~が気になる、心配だ／**waistline** = ウエスト、胴回り／**exceed** = 超える／**standard for ~** = ~の基準／**overweight** = 太りすぎ／**obesity** = 肥満 cf. skinny = やせすぎ

「メタボ」metabolic syndrome は医学用語なので、日常では一般的にあまり使われない。

What a shock! = ビックリだ!／**eyesight** = 視力 cf. have good(bad) eyesight = 視力がいい（悪い）／**get worse** = 悪くなる（worseはbad<悪い>の比較級）

「眼鏡なしで視力はどれくらいですか？」と言うには What's your eyesight like without your glasses on?。

---

be relieved = ホッとする、安心する／**result of ~** = ~の結果／**medical checkup** = 健康診断

I'm glad to know that the results of the checkup haven't changed from last year.（結果が変わっていないのを知ってうれしい）と言ってもよい。

Skit 社内行事編

気もお金も遣います、社内交流も楽じゃない

Man: **Did you go to the company cherry-blossom-viewing party? I didn't see you.**

Woman: **No, I had to organize the farewell party for Masako.**

M: **It was fun. I made a toast that everyone enjoyed.**

W: **Did you have to pour the manager's beer?**

M: **Yes, but he's totally different once he gets drunk. He was very funny.**

W: **I'm sorry I missed❶ it. Hey, are you going to attend Hiroshi's wedding reception?**

M: **Yes, and thanks for reminding❷❸ me. I have to pick up an envelope for his gift money.**

W: **How much money should I give?**

M: **I think ¥30,000 will be enough❹. His❺ will be the third company wedding this year. It's expensive coming up with all that gift money.**

W: **I have to make a congratulatory speech at the wedding but I don't know him that well.**

M: **Let's have lunch together. I'll help❻ you write it.**

W: **Thanks!**

男性：会社の花見に参加した？ 君のこと見かけなかったんだけど。
女性：行かなかったわ。雅子の送別会の幹事だったものだから。
男：花見は楽しかったよ。乾杯して回ったんだけど、みんな喜んでくれて。
女：部長にお酌もしなきゃならなかったんじゃない？
男：そうなんだけど、でも部長って酔うと別人だね。すっごく面白かった。
女：私も見たかったわあ。ところで、弘の結婚披露宴には出る？
男：そうだ、おかげで思い出したよ。ご祝儀袋用意しなきゃいけなかったんだ。
女：いくら出せばいいのかしら？
男：3万円で十分だと思うよ。これで今年の会社がらみの結婚式は3件目だ。全部合わせるとご祝儀がきついなあ。
女：私、結婚式でスピーチをしなきゃいけないんだけど、彼のことそんなに知らないのよねえ。
男：一緒にランチに行こうよ。スピーチの原稿書き手伝うから。
女：ありがとう！

【語注】

❶ miss: 見落とす、見そこなう、聞きそこなう
❷ thanks for ~ing: 〜してくれてありがとう
❸ remind: 〜に思い出させる
❹ enough: 十分な
❺ his: =his wedding
❻ help – ...: 〜が…するのを手伝う

Quick Check

本章に出てきたフレーズを復習しましょう。以下の日本語の意味になるよう英文を完成させてください。答えはページの下にあります。

❶親睦会の手配をする。 ➡P212
I ( ) a ( ) meeting.

❷ネットで送別会用の店を探す。 ➡P213
On the Internet, I look for a restaurant for the ( ) ( ).

❸ゴルフの社内コンペに出る。 ➡P213
I ( ) the company golf ( ).

❹研修を受ける。 ➡P214
I get ( ) ( ).

❺今度のプロジェクトが落ち着いたら、部署のみんなでパーッと飲みに行こう。 ➡P216
When this project ( ) ( ), let's all go drinking and have some ( )!

❻みんなの予定がなかなか合わない。 ➡P216
It's difficult for everyone to ( ) ( ) ( ) ( ).

❼斎藤さんが部長に絡んでる。無礼講って真に受けちゃだめだよ。 ➡P216
Mr. Saito is ( ) ( ) with the boss. He shouldn't ( ) "*bureiko*" ( ) ( ) ( ) and ignore rank and manners.

❽忘年会続きで体がもたないよ。 ➡P218
I don't ( ) ( ) I can ( ) all these year-end parties.

❾忘年会の出し物、今年は何にするかなあ、頭が痛いよ。 ➡P220
What kind of party ( ) should I do for the year-end party? It's a ( ) ( ) ( ) ( ).

❿ボーリング大会の参加は必須でなく任意です。 ➡P220
It's ( ) ( ) ( ) whether you ( ) ( ) ( ) the bowling ( ); it's not ( ).

---

❶arrange or organize/get-acquainted ❷farewell/party ❸enter/competition ❹on-the-job/training ❺settles/down/fun ❻agree/on/the/schedule ❼picking/fights/take/at/face/value ❽know/if/survive ❾trick/pain/in/the/neck ❿up/to/you/take/part/in/tournament/obligatory

chapter 9
人事・待遇
Personnel Matters

雇用形態、人事評価、給与、異動、
といった労働環境に関するさまざまな
用語や表現を取り上げました。
会社員にとっては死活問題ですから、
喜怒哀楽に富んだ心のつぶやきも
増そうというものです。

chapter 9 Personnel Matters

Words 単語編

❶ 正社員
❷ 派遣スタッフ
❸ 派遣会社
❹ 嘱託
❺ 採用
❻ 人事部
❼ 人事評価
❽ 自己評価
❾ 業績
❿ 能力主義
⓫ 年休
⓬ 有休
⓭ 産休／育休
⓮ 傷病休暇
⓯ 労働環境

❶permanent employee ❷temp staff ❸temporary-employment agency ❹temporary worker ❺recruitment ❻personnel department ❼personnel evaluation ❽self-evaluation ❾business performance ❿ability-based system ⓫annual paid holiday

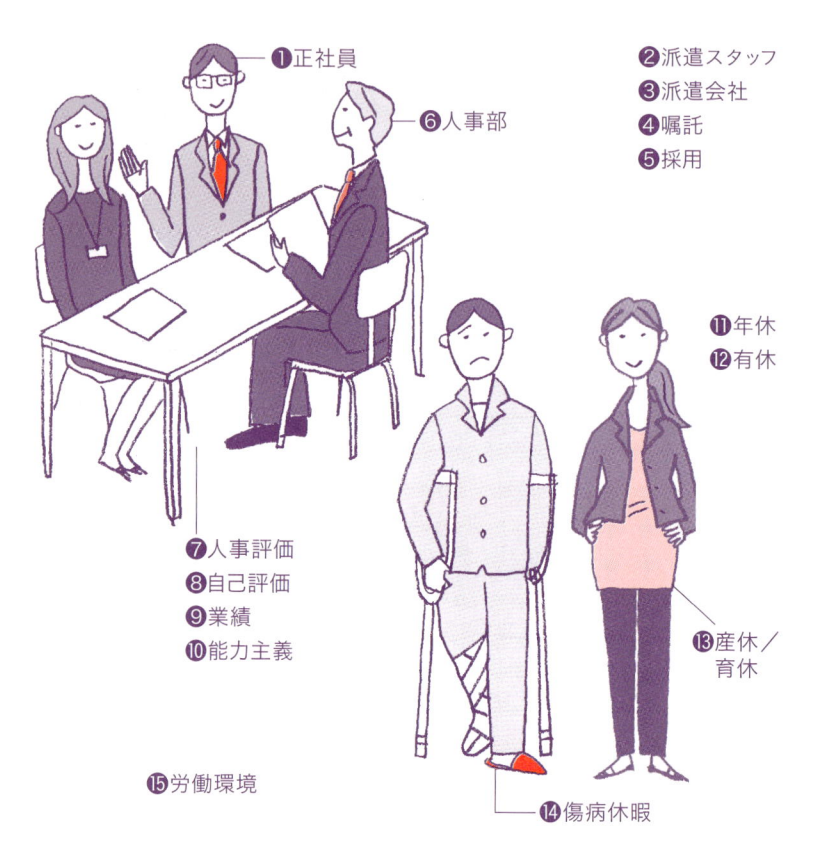

まずは、さまざまな物や事の名前で
「人事・待遇」のシーンのイメージをつかもう。

⑯給料
⑰ボーナス
⑱年俸制

⑲昇進
⑳降格
㉑出世争い

㉒昇給
㉓減給

㉔退職願

㉕早期退職
㉖終身雇用

⑫paid <u>day off/holiday</u>　⑬maternity leave　⑭medical leave　⑮ working environment　⑯pay　⑰bonus　⑱annual salary system　⑲promotion　⑳demotion　㉑rat race　㉒pay raise　㉓pay cut　㉔ letter of resignation　㉕early retirement　㉖permanent employment

chapter 9 Personnel Matters

1 パートで働く
I work part-time.

2 時短で働く
I work shorter hours.

3 週に3日、在宅勤務する
I work at home three days a week.

4 派遣会社に登録する
I sign up with a temporary-employment agency.

5 企業に派遣される
I am dispatched to a company.

tips

❶ work on a part-time basis、work as a part-timerでもよい。
❸「[電話やネットを使って]在宅勤務する」はdo telecommuting。
❹「派遣会社」はstaffing companyとも言う。
❻ I terminate my contract with the company.で「その会社との契約を解除する」。

6 1年ごとに派遣の契約を更新する
I renew my temporary contract every year.

7 ワークシェアする
I share the workload with colleagues.

8 嘱託で会社に残る
I continue to work as a temporary worker after retirement.

9 フレックス制で働く
I work flextime.

10 完全週休2日制で働く
I take two days off every week.

❽「一定の時期、正社員同様に勤務する人（嘱託社員）」はtemporary worker、「特定の曜日・時間だけ勤務する人」はpart-time worker。
❾work a flexible schedule / flexible hours とも言う。
❿「会社は週休2日制です」はMy company has a five-day workweek system. と言う。

chapter 9 Personnel Matters

11 午前休を取る
I take the morning off.

12 有休(年休)を完全消化する
I use all my <u>paid days off</u> (<u>annual paid holidays</u>).

13 産休(育休)を取る
I take maternity leave.

14 残業する
I work <u>overtime/after hours</u>.

15 上司に残業申請する
I apply for permission from my boss to work overtime.

tips

⓫「土曜はいつも半休です」は We work a half day on Saturdays.。
⓬ I'm on a paid holiday today. で「今日は有休を取っています」。
⓭「産休」も「育休」も maternity leave で表す。男性が「育休」を取る場合は paternity leave と言う。「産休(育休)から復帰する」は return to work after taking maternity leave。

16 休日出勤する
I come to work on a holiday.

17 労働環境の改善を求める
I request improvements in my/our working environment.

18 人事面談を受ける
I have an interview with the personnel department.

19 昇進(昇給)する
I get a promotion (pay raise).

⓮ 概して overtime は「残業代が支払われる超過勤務」、after hours はいわゆる「サービス残業」を指す。
⓯ cut back on unnecessary overtime で「無駄な残業を減らす」。
⓲ 「人事権を握っている」は have the power to shuffle personnel。
⓳ 「降格になる」は suffer a demotion、「減給になる」は take pay cuts。

chapter 9 Personnel Matters

20 評価に異議を申し立てる
I question my evaluation.

21 自己評価のフィードバックを受ける
I receive feedback about the self-evaluation.

22 異動願いを出す
I request a transfer.

23 9月1日付で販売部へ異動になる
I'll be transferred to the sales department as of September 1.

24 関連会社に出向する
I work temporarily at an affiliate company.

tips

⑳「〜に満足している」はbe happy with 〜。 e.g. I'm happy with my evaluation.（評価に満足しています）
㉑「自己評価シート」はself-evaluation form/questionnaire。
㉒「退職届」はletter of resignation。 e.g. I submitted a letter of resignation.（退職届を提出しました）

25 異動に伴いあいさつ回りをする
I'm transferred to a new workplace, and make courtesy visits to the staff there.

26 気に入らない部下を飛ばす
I send off <u>an employee</u> / <u>a worker</u> I don't get along with.

27 肩たたきされる
I'm pressured into early retirement.

28 チームリーダーに抜擢される
I'm selected as team leader.

㉔「子会社」は subsidiary company と言う。
㉕「あいさつ回りをする」は go the rounds of courtesy calls でもよい。
㉖ be sent off to ~ で「~に飛ばされる」。e.g. My boss was sent off to the Okinawa branch.(上司は沖縄営業所に飛ばされた)
㉗「窓際族[の社員]」は deadwood employee と言う。

chapter 9 Personnel Matters

1. 私には派遣という働き方が性に合ってる。
I sure have a bent for temping.

2. 彼女は派遣だけど、下手すると正社員より働いてる。
She's a temp staff but she might work more than a permanent employee.

3. 出来ない上司のしわ寄せはもうたくさん！
That's it. I can't take working under my lousy boss any more.

4. 契約時の説明と実際の業務内容が違うんですけど。
What? The explanation at the time of the contract signing doesn't seem to conform to the actual job duties.

5. あの派遣社員さん、うちの社員になる気ないかな。
I wonder if that temp staff wants to join us full time.

6. 正社員だからって、安心していられない世の中だね。
Even permanent employees don't feel assured of permanent employment these days.

have a bent for ~ = ~が性に合う、~に向いている／temp(= work as a temporary worker) = 派遣社員として働く

「性に合わない、向いていない」は not cut out for ~ を使う。e.g. I don't think I'm cut out for accounting.（自分は会計に向いてないみたいだ）

---

temp staff = 派遣社員、嘱託社員(temp = temporary)／permanent employee = 正社員

「正社員」の反対に当たる語は「パート（part-timer）」。e.g. The company needs to lower the barrier between full-timers and part-timers.（会社はフルタイムの社員とパートの間にある仕切りを下げるべきだ）

That's it. = そこまでだ!(強い不満を表す)／can't take ~ any more = これ以上~を我慢できない／lousy = いやな、卑劣な、ひどい

「[失敗の] 尻ぬぐいをする」は reap（収穫する）を使って reap the harvest of someone's mistakes。 e.g. The manager reaped the harvest of his staff's mistakes.（部長は部下の失敗の尻ぬぐいをした）

---

seem to ~ = ~するように見える／conform to ~ = ~に一致する／job duties = 職務内容、職務上の義務

That's totally different from what I heard! で「聞いていた内容と全然違うよ！」。「内容」は content を使って、job content（職務内容）、business content（業務内容）のように言うこともできる。

I wonder if ~ = ~だろうか、~かな／join = ~に入る(usは会社のこと)／full time = フルタイムで、常勤で

「~を登用する」は promote。e.g. We're actively promoting women in the sales department.（当社販売部では積極的に女性を登用しています）

---

feel assured of ~ = ~について安心できる／permanent employment = 終身雇用

「雇用不安」を employment insecurity と言う。e.g. Have you ever felt stressed about employment insecurity?（雇用不安に対してストレスを感じたことがありますか）

chapter 9 Personnel Matters

7 今年は一斉採用はなしだ。
We won't do any mass recruitment this year.

8 連休は嬉しいけど、時給で働く身にはつらいんだよね……。
Of course I'm happy with consecutive holidays, but, sadly enough, an hourly-wage worker like me doesn't get paid for them.

9 待ちに待った給料日だ。
Today is payday. I've really been looking forward to it.

10 あ、それは手取りじゃなくて額面だから。
Oh, that's not after-tax but before-tax, I might add.

11 こんなに税金取られてるなんて悔しい。
It's so frustrating just to know this much tax is deducted from my paycheck.

12 不景気のあおりで、社員一律5パーセントの減給だって！
Every employee's going to have their salary cut by 5 percent because of the on-going recession? This is ridiculous!

mass recruitment = 一斉採用

mass は「大量の、集団の」の意味。「新卒採用」は graduate recruitment、「[時期的な] 中途採用」は intermediate recruitment、「[キャリアのある人の] 中途採用」は mid-career recruitment と言う。

---

consecutive holidays = 連休／sadly enough = 悲しいことに／hourly-wage = 時間給で働く／get paid for ~ = ~に対して給料が支払われる

get paid by the hour で「時給で支払われる」。e.g. Students get paid by the hour at ¥800.（学生は時給 800 円です）

---

payday = 給料日／look forward to ~ = ~を楽しみにする

I can hardly wait for payday. で「給料日が待ち遠しい」。なお、米国紙幣には鷲（ワシ）が描かれていることから、アメリカでは給料日を when the eagle flies というスラングがある。

---

after-tax = 税引き後の、手取りの／before-tax = 税引き前の

I might add は「~と一言付け加えておきます、ちなみに」と付加情報を述べる際に使うフレーズ。「所得税」は income tax、「手取りの給料」は take-home（家に持ち帰るもの）のように言う。

---

frustrating = 悔しい、イライラする／this much ~ = これだけたくさんの~／be deducted from ~ = ~から差し引かれる／paycheck = 給与（支払い小切手）

「天引きされる」は automatically（自動的に）を使って、Income tax is automatically deducted from pay.（所得税は給料から自動的に天引きされます）のように言う。

---

have ~ cut = ~をカットされる／on-going = 現在進行中の／recession = 不景気／ridiculous = ばかげた、とんでもない

景気が悪い状態を示す類義語には depression（恐慌、不況）、downturn（経済の停滞）、slowdown（景気後退）などがある。This is ridiculous! は、This is unbelievable!（信じられない）と言ってもよい。

chapter 9 Personnel Matters

13 この給料じゃどう見ても割に合わないよ。
Is this all I get for my job? Obviously, what I do is worth more than this!

---

14 給料も下がったし、本業のほかにバイトでもしようかなあ。
Maybe I should start moonlighting, since my salary was reduced.

---

15 初ボーナスで、田舎の両親に何か送ろうかな。
How about buying something for my parents back home with my first bonus?

---

16 このままじゃ、冬のボーナスは望み薄だな。
Unless things turn around, we won't get much of a winter bonus.

---

17 このご時世に、ボーナスが出るだけでもありがたい。
The good thing is that I get to receive a bonus at a time like this.

---

18 業績が上がったから、特別ボーナス出るって！
You know what, we'll get a special bonus because our business performance has improved.

obviously, ~ = どう見ても~だ／worth more than ~ = ~以上の価値がある

「この仕事は割に合わない」は This job doesn't pay. と言う。pay は「利益になる、苦労が報われる」の意味。また、The game is not worth the candle.（骨折り損のくたびれもうけ）ということわざもある。

---

moonlight = アルバイトする／reduce = 縮小する

moonlight は動詞で「[副職として主に夜に] 掛け持ちの仕事をする」の意味。月明かりの中でこっそり仕事をする様子から来ている。

How about ~ing? = ~するのはどうだろうか／back home = 故郷の

「ボーナスをもらう」は get/receive a bonus。e.g. I got a big bonus this year.（今年はボーナスがたくさん出た）、We receive a bonus twice a year.（ボーナスは年 2 回支給されます）、I'll pay for it out of my winter bonus.（冬のボーナスで一括払いしよう）

---

unless ~ = ~でなければ／things = 状況／turn around = 好転する

turn around の名詞形 turnaround には「好転、営業の黒字化」という意味がある。e.g. We've achieved a turnaround this year.（今年度当社は業績黒字を達成しました／赤字から黒字に転じました）

---

get to ~ = ~する特権がある、~できる機会がある

The good thing is [that] ~ は、「よい面は~です」の意味。似た表現に The thing is ~（要は、問題となるのは~）がある。e.g. The thing is we can't move on to the next stage.（要は次の段階に進めないということなのです）

You know what, = あのね（相手の注意を喚起するフレーズ）／performance = 業績／improve = 改善する

相手の注意を喚起するフレーズはほかに、興味深い話をふる際の Guess what.（ちょっと聞いてよ、何だと思う？）、相手の行動に助言する際の Tell you what.（いいですか、聞いてください）などがある。

chapter 9 Personnel Matters

19 ボーナスはローンと生活費の補填で終わり……。
My bonus will be spent on loans and living expenses only.

20 うちの会社は年俸制だ。
Our company adopts the annual salary system.

21 管理職は、残業代がもらえない。
Managers don't get paid for overtime work.

22 今日はノー残業デーだ。
Hooray! It's a no-overtime day today.

23 残った有休と夏期休暇を合わせて、まとまった休みを取ろうかな。
I think I'm going to make it a long vacation by combining the unused paid holidays with regular summer holidays.

24 有休がなかなか取得できなくて毎年何日も捨ててるよ。
I just can't take a paid holiday. I have to give up using them up.

CD 2
15

be spent on ~ = ~に費やされる／living expenses = 生活費
expenses（費用）の代表的なものとしては、food expenses（食費）、heating and electricity expenses（光熱費）、traffic expenses（交通費）、medical expenses（医療費）、educational expenses（教育費）、entertainment expenses（交際費）などがある。

---

adopt ~ = ~を採用している／annual = 年次の、年1回の
We are paid on an annual basis in the company. でもほぼ同じ意味。on ~ basis で「~に基づいて、~ベースで」。e.g. I write e-mail in English on a daily basis.（毎日のように英語でメールを書いています）

---

manager =［部長など］管理職／get paid for ~ = ~の対価を支払われる／overtime work = 残業
「残業手当」は overtime allowance/premium、「サービス残業」は unpaid overtime（無給の超過勤務）または off-the-clock work（勤務時間外の仕事）などと言う。

Hooray! = やった!／no-overtime = 残業のない
「定時に退社する」は leave the office on time。e.g. Why don't we leave the office on time and have a drink?（定時に退社して一杯やろうか）

---

combine ~ with ... = ~と…を合わせる／unused = 未使用の
有休を「残しておく、とっておく」は conserve を使う。e.g. It's still June, so I'd better conserve sick leave.（まだ6月だから、病気のための有休を残しておかないとまずいな）

---

give up ~ing = ~するのをあきらめる／use ~ up = ~を使い切る
「有休を完全消化する」は I use all my paid days off/holidays。「[有休を]持ち越す」は carry over ~。e.g. I don't know how many paid holidays I can carry over.（有休は何日持ち越せるかわからない）

chapter 9 Personnel Matters

25 傷病休暇の申請には診断書が必要だ。
You need a doctor's certificate to apply for medical leave.

26 仕事仕事の人生はいやだ。ワークライフバランスを大切にしたい。
I hate to spend my life working all the time. I want to value the balance of work and life.

27 マーブリー社ではいまだに育休取るといい顔されないんだって。
They say taking maternity leave is still frowned upon at Marbley.

28 最近は、男性でも育休を取る人が増えてきた。世の中変わったなあ。
More and more men are taking paternity leave these days. It's a whole different world.

29 明日から産休に入ります。その間ご迷惑をお掛けしますが、よろしくお願いします。
I'm going on maternity leave tomorrow. I hope it won't cause you any inconvenience.

30 終身雇用制は昔の話。今は能力主義が浸透してきた。
Permanent employment is already a thing of the past. Nowadays, ability-based systems have become widespread.

doctor's certificate = 医師の診断書／medical leave = 傷病休暇

apply for ~ は「~を申請する、申し込む」の意味。e.g. apply for unemployment benefits(a tax deduction)（失業給付金＜税金の控除＞を申請する）。なお、claim workers' compensation（労災を申請する）のように claim（請求する）を使う場合もある。

---

hate to ~ = ~するのは嫌だ／value ~ = ~を重視する

All work and no play makes Jack a dull boy.（よく学びよく遊べ）ということわざがあるが、「仕事しかしていない人」を all-work-no-play person と呼ぶ。「仕事中毒の社員」は workaholic employee、または compulsive worker と言う。

---

be frowned upon = 嫌な顔をされる

be frowned upon（ひんしゅくを買う、冷たい目で見られる）の frown は「しかめ面[する]」の意味。e.g. Drinking on the street is not illegal, but it is frowned upon, you know.（路上で飲むのは違法じゃないけど、ひんしゅくを買うよね）

---

more and more ~ = ますます多くの~／paternity leave = 育児休暇／whole different = 完全に別の

paternity は「父親の」という意味。よって paternity leave は「[父親が取る]育児休暇」のこと。「[母親の]出産・育児休暇」は maternity leave と言う。「世の中変わってきてるね」は Things are changing.。

---

go on ~ = ~に入る／cause you ~ = あなたに[不便や苦痛など]をもたらす／inconvenience = 不都合、迷惑

inconvenience（不便）は動詞で「~に迷惑をかける」の意味がある。e.g. I hope I didn't inconvenience you in my absence.（私が不在の間、ご不便をおかけしていなければいいのですが）

---

permanent employment = 終身雇用／a thing of the past = 過去のもの／ability-based = 能力に基づく／widespread = 広く知られた

「年功序列制」は seniority system と言う。e.g. Japanese companies are gradually phasing out the seniority system.（現在、日本の企業は段階的に年功序列制を廃止しています）

chapter 9 Personnel Matters

31 評価の根拠が曖昧で、納得がいかないよ。
The basis for the evaluation result is so vague I can't go along with it.

32 彼の人事評価はちょっと甘すぎるんじゃないか。どこを見てるんだ。
Isn't he a bit too lenient in personnel evaluations? I wonder what he <u>looks at</u> / <u>takes into account</u>.

33 彼女は自己評価が高すぎるんだよなあ。
She thinks too highly of herself, doesn't she?

34 仕事は抱え込まないで、もっと部下にふらなきゃ。
Don't take a lot of tasks at once. You should leave some of them to your staff.

35 もっと営業らしい仕事をさせてください！
Do you think you could give me more jobs as a salesperson?

36 うつ病って、ずいぶん身近な病気になったんだなあ。
Depression sure has become a disease that's close to home.

basis for ~ = ~の根拠／vague = 曖昧な／can't go along with ~ = ~に納得がいかない(go along with ~は「~に同調する」)

相手に「根拠」を問う言い方としては、What do you base that on?（その根拠は何ですか）、On what grounds do you say that?（何を根拠にそんなことを言うのですか）などがある。

---

a bit too ~ = ちょっと~すぎる／lenient = 寛大な、甘い／personnel evaluation = 人事評価／take ~ into account = ~を考慮に入れる

「[採点や評価が] 甘い」には lenient または generous（寛大な）を使う。e.g. I think you'll pass the interview because he is a generous grader.（彼は評価が甘いから、面接は大丈夫だと思うよ）

---

think highly of ~ = ~を高く評価する

「自己評価する」は evaluate oneself、「自己評価」は self-evaluation と言うのが一般的。ここでは「自尊心」(self-esteem) のことを述べているので、Her self-esteem is too high, isn't it ? と言うこともできる。

---

at once = 一度に、同時に／leave ~ to ... = ~を…に任せる

「仕事を~にふる」は assign a job to ~ でもよい。「同僚と仕事を分け合う」は I share my workload with colleagues.。work-sharing（仕事を分け合うこと）は広く知られた語。e.g. We've adopted a work-sharing system.（当社はワークシェアリングを採用しました）

---

as ~ = ~として

treat someone as ~（人を~として扱う）を使って、Will you treat me as a salesperson?（営業担当者として扱ってください）のようにも言える。「適した」は suitable。e.g. This job isn't suitable for me.（この仕事は自分には合っていない）

---

depression = うつ病／disease = 病気／be close to home = 身近な

close to home は「家に近い」つまり「自分になじみのある」という意味。e.g. Let's begin close to home.（手近なところから始めよう）、I got hit close to home and couldn't say a word.（痛いところを突かれてぐうの音も出なかった）

chapter 9 Personnel Matters

37 彼は同期の出世頭だ。
He's the most up-and-coming among my peers.

---

38 この部署にいる限り、出世は望めない。
As long as I work here in this department, the chances are slim that I'll get a promotion.

---

39 出世争いのごたごたはごめんだ。
I really want to stay out of the rat race.

---

40 今の部署も長いし、自分の可能性を広げる意味でも異動したいなあ。
I've been working in the department for so long I want to transfer to somewhere different to open up some new possibilities.

---

41 これって、栄転？ それとも左遷？
Is this a promotion or a demotion?

---

42 来春の人事で、部長栄転で本社だって。
From what I heard, the manager is expected to be promoted and transferred to the main office next spring.

up-and-coming = 将来有望な、野心的な／peer = 同期、同僚

「出世頭だ」は promising（有望な）と表現することもできる。up-and-coming のもとになった come up は「成功する」の意味。e.g. I'll come up in the world some day.（いつか出世するぞ）

---

as long as ~ = ~の限りは／chances are slim that ~ = ~の見込みはほとんどない／get a promotion = 昇進する

chances は「可能性、見込み」の意味。Chances are that ~（たぶん~だろう）は会話でよく使う表現。e.g. Chances are that the guy will be transferred.（たぶんあいつは転勤させられるだろう）

---

stay out of ~ = ~にかかわらない／rat race = 出世争い

「出世街道、出世コース」は fast lane と言う。e.g. Josh's trying hard to get into the fast lane in the company.（ジョッシュは会社の出世コースに乗ろうと必死だ）

---

transfer to ~ = ~へ異動する／open up = [可能性などを]開花させる／possibility = 可能性

「潜在的な能力」は one's potential と言う。e.g. I need to fully exert my potential to tackle the difficult task.（その難題に取り組むには自分の潜在能力をフルに発揮する必要がある）

---

promotion = 昇進、栄転／demotion = 降格、左遷

be promoted/demoted to ~ で「~に昇進（降格）させられる」。e.g. Mr. Hemans was demoted to assistant manager.（ヘマンズさんは課長補佐へと降格させられた）。また、get a promotion（昇進する）、suffer a demotion（降格する）という言い方もある。

---

be expected to ~ = ~すると見込まれている／main office = 本社

from what I heard は「聞くところによると」という意味。「うわさで~を聞く」は hear ~ through/on the grapevine。grapevine は「ブドウのつる」、転じて「情報源」。e.g. I heard this on the grapevine — she's getting married.（うわさで聞いたんだけど、彼女結婚するんだって）

chapter 9 Personnel Matters

43 寝耳に水の人事異動だ。
This sure is an out-of-the-blue transfer.

44 家を買ったら転勤になるって本当だったんだねえ……。
It actually turned out to be true that you get a company transfer right after purchasing a new home.

45 単身赴任するしかないかなあ。
I guess I have no choice but to live away from home for work.

46 転勤が決まって、彼女と遠距離に……。
Because of the company transfer I got, I'm going to have to have a long-distance relationship with my girlfriend.

47 畑違いの部署に異動になったよ。
I'm going to transfer to a department out of my field.

48 つまるところ、出世するのはイエスマンかあ。
Seriously, only brown-nosers can move up the ladder.

out-of-the-blue = 予告なしの、不意の

「寝耳に水」は a bolt out of the blue（青空 <blue sky> から突然稲妻 <thunderbolt> が出現すること）と言う。e.g. The news that she got pregnant was a real bolt out of the blue.（彼女に子どもができたという知らせは全くもって寝耳に水だった）

---

turn out ~ = 結局~だとわかる／right after ~ = ~の直後に

transfer（転勤）の了承に関する表現としては、I accept the company transfer without complaining.（不平不満を言わずに転勤を受け入れる）、I decline the transfer for the sake of my family.（家族のために転勤を断る）などがある。

---

have no choice but to ~ = ~するほかに選択の余地がない

英語で「単身赴任」に該当する語句がないので、live away from home for work（仕事のため家庭から離れて生活する）と表現する。「選択の余地がない[のであきらめて]」は There is no choice.。

---

long-distance relationship with ~ = ~との遠距離の関係

「遠距離恋愛」は文字通り long-distance love でも OK。e.g. We miss out on seeing each other because of our long-distance love.（遠距離恋愛のせいでお互い会う機会を逃しています）

---

out of one's field = 自分とは分野が違う、畑違いの

「場違いの人間」を魚にたとえて、fish out of water（水から出てしまった魚）と言う。e.g. I've been feeling like a fish out of water in this department.（この部署ではずっと自分は場違いなような気がしている）

---

seriously = 本当のところ／brown-noser = ゴマをする人／move up the ladder = 出世階段を上る

「イエスマン」つまり「ゴマをする人」は brown-noser と言う。apple-polisher（リンゴを磨く人）とも言うが、最近では軽蔑して kiss-ass などのように呼ぶ（使う相手に注意）。

chapter 9 Personnel Matters

49 出向先で優しく受け入れてくれるか心配だ。
I'm concerned whether I'll be welcome at the new workplace where I'm going to be working temporarily.

50 後任のために、引き継ぎ資料を作っておいた方がいいな。
I think I should prepare some materials for the person taking over my job.

51 彼、ひそかに転職活動してるらしいよ。
I heard that he's trying to switch companies on the sly.

52 あんなに仕事中毒で、退職後はどうするんだろう。
I wonder what he's going to do after retirement; he's such a workaholic.

53 部内で業務替えが発表された。
A switch of job duties was announced in the department.

54 上司がアメリカ人になって、仕事にメリハリができたな。
I get to vary the pace of my work performance since an American became my boss.

be concerned whether ~ = ～かどうか心配している

「～に出向する」は be on loan to ~ という言い方もあるが、これは派遣元の視点から見た硬い言い方（「～へ貸出中」の意味）なので、実際に働く側は work temporarily（[派遣されて]一時的に勤務する）と言えばよい。

---

material = 資料／take over ~ = ～を引き継ぐ

「[役職の]後任」は replacement と言う。「A が B の後任となる」は B be replaced by A と表現する。e.g. Mr. Maeda has been replaced by Mr. Goto.（後藤さんが前田さんの後任になりました）

---

switch ~ = ～を換える／on the sly = ひそかに

「ひそかに、陰で」を意味する語句には secretly、behind someone's back（～の陰で）などがあるが、like a thief in the night（闇夜に働く盗賊のように）は面白い表現。e.g. He snuck out of the meeting like a thief in the night.（彼はひそかに会議を抜け出した：snuck は sneak ＜こっそり立ち去る＞の過去・過去分詞形）

---

retirement = 退職／workaholic = 仕事中毒の人

「定年退職」は age-limit/compulsory retirement。「退職後に趣味を始める」は take up a hobby after retirement、「[日光浴などをして]退職後に悠々自適の生活を送る」は bask in retirement と言う。

---

switch = 転換／job duties = 業務、職務

job duties は「[仕事上の]職責、職務、業務」のこと。e.g. My job duties are going to double my present responsibilities.（業務は現在の職務の倍になるだろう）。「業務引継ぎ作業」は handover process と言う。

---

get to ~ = ～する機会がある／vary the pace = ペースを変える、メリハリをつける

「[新しいことが]空気を変える」は change the atmosphere。e.g. The new secretary completely changed the atmosphere of the office.（新しい秘書のおかげで職場の空気がガラッと変わった）

Skit 人事・待遇編

こんなの変！ 人事評価に異議あり！

Woman: That's it. I can't take working under my lousy boss any more.

Man: What's the problem?①

W: I'm questioning my evaluation. The basis for it is so vague, I just can't agree with it.

M: Can't you talk to him about it?

W: I tried but his explanation doesn't make any sense②. Also, I work overtime almost every day③ but I never get a promotion.

M: These days, you should be glad④ you have a job at all⑤.

W: I know that, but I've been working in the department so long... I want to transfer to somewhere different to open up new possibilities.

M: Can you request a transfer?

W: I have an interview with the personnel department tomorrow.

M: What if⑥ they won't give you a transfer⑦?

W: Maybe I'll quit⑧ and work part time. I could work shorter hours and spend more time with my family.

女性：もういや！ あんなひどいボスの下で働くのはこれ以上がまんできないわ！
男性：どうしたの？
女：私に対する評価がおかしいのよ。評価基準があいまいで、納得できないわ。
男：ボスとそのことについて話し合えないの？
女：話し合ってみたんだけど、彼の説明ったら全く意味不明なの。それに、ほとんど毎日残業してるのに、全然昇進できないんだから。
男：このご時世で、仕事があるってだけでもありがたいと思わなきゃ。
女：わかってるわよ。でもねえ、この部署も長いのよねえ、可能性を広げる意味でも、どこか別の部署に異動したいわ。
男：異動願い出せるの？
女：明日、人事部との面談があるの。
男：もし異動できなかったらどうするつもり？
女：辞めてパートタイムで働くわ。時短で働けば、家族との時間も増やせるしね。

【語注】

❶ What's the problem?: どうしましたか、何があったのですか
❷ not make any sense: 全く意味をなさない、さっぱりわからない、理にかなっていない
❸ almost every day: ほぼ毎日
❹ you should be glad: 満足すべきだ、感謝すべきだ
❺ at all: とにかく（肯定文の場合）
❻ What if ~?: もし〜だったらどうしますか
❼ give ~ a transfer: 〜を異動させる
❽ quit: 辞職する

Quick Check

本章に出てきたフレーズを復習しましょう。以下の日本語の意味になるよう英文を完成させてください。答えはページの下にあります。

❶派遣会社に登録する。 ➡P232
I (　　　) (　　　　) with a temporary-employment agency.

❷私には派遣という働き方が性に合ってる。 ➡P238
I sure have (　　　) (　　　　) (　　　　) temping.

❸明日から産休に入ります。その間ご迷惑をお掛けしますが、よろしくお願いします。 ➡P246
I'm going on (　　　　) (　　　　) tomorrow. I hope it won't (　　　　) you any (　　　　).

❹終身雇用制は昔の話。今は能力主義が浸透してきた。 ➡P246
(　　　) employment is already a (　　　　) of (　　　) (　　　　).
Nowadays, (　　　) systems have become (　　　　).

❺彼は同期の出世頭だ。 ➡P250
He's the most (　　　　) among my peers.

❻この部署にいる限り、出世は望めない。 ➡P250
(　　) (　　　) (　　　　) I work here in this department, the (　　　　) (　　　) (　　　) that I'll get a (　　　　).

❼出世争いのごたごたはごめんだ。 ➡P250
I really want to (　　　) (　　　) (　　　　) the (　　　) (　　　).

❽寝耳に水の人事異動だ。 ➡P252
This sure is an (　　　　) (　　　　).

❾つまるところ、出世するのはイエスマンかぁ。 ➡P252
Seriously, only (　　　) can (　　　) (　　　) the (　　　).

❿あんなに仕事中毒で、退職後はどうするんだろう。 ➡P254
I wonder what he's going to do after (　　　　); he's such a (　　　　).

---

❶sign/up ❷a/bent/for ❸maternity/leave/cause/inconvenience ❹Permanent/thing/the/past/ability-based/widespread ❺up-and-coming ❻As/long/as/chances/are/slim/promotion ❼stay/out/of/rat/race ❽out-of-the-blue/transfer ❾brown-nosers/move/up/ladder ❿retirement/workaholic

chapter 10
アフター5
After-Work Hours

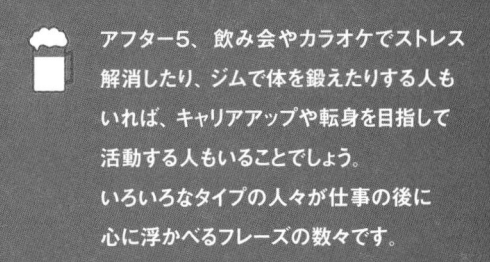

アフター5、飲み会やカラオケでストレス解消したり、ジムで体を鍛えたりする人もいれば、キャリアアップや転身を目指して活動する人もいることでしょう。
いろいろなタイプの人々が仕事の後に心に浮かべるフレーズの数々です。

chapter 10 After-Work Hours

Words 単語編

❶飲み会
❷居酒屋
❸屋台
❹はしご酒
❺二日酔い
❻合コン
❼オフ会
❽カラオケ
❾マイク
❿リモコン

❶drinking session ❷tavern ❸food stall ❹bar-hopping ❺hangover ❻mixer ❼off-line meeting ❽karaoke ❾microphone ❿remote control ⓫cross-industrial exchange meeting ⓬study session ⓭seminar outside the company ⓮computer training

まずは、さまざまな物や事の名前で
「アフター5」のシーンのイメージをつかもう。

⑪異業種交流会
⑫勉強会
⑬社外セミナー
⑭パソコン教室
⑮中国語教室
⑯習い事
⑰資格試験
⑱副業
⑲ボランティア活動
⑳ライブ
㉑芝居
㉒ネイルサロン
㉓エステ
㉔美容室
㉕マッサージ屋さん
㉖ヨガ教室
㉗ジム／スポーツクラブ

⑪networking party ⑫study meeting ⑬external seminar ⑭computer school ⑮Chinese-language class ⑯lessons ⑰certification exam ⑱second job ⑲volunteer work ⑳concert ㉑play ㉒nail salon ㉓esthetic clinic ㉔beauty salon ㉕massage parlor ㉖yoga class ㉗gym

chapter 10 After-Work Hours

1 飲み会に同僚を誘う
I ask my colleague out for a drink.

2 飲んで憂さを晴らす
I drink away my troubles.

3 ヤケ食いする
I go on eating binges.

4 飲み屋をはしごする
I go bar hopping.

5 4対4の合コンをセットする
I set up a mixer for four men and four women.

tips

❶ ask 〜 out で「〜を誘う」、ask out for lunch なら「ランチに誘う」、ask out for a date で「デートに誘う」。
❷ drink away で「酒を飲んで[心配事を]忘れようとする」。
❸ binge は「好きなだけ飲み食べること」。「食べすぎ」は overeating。
❹ hopping は「次から次へと移動すること」。

6 合コンの人数合わせをする
I arrange the same number of men and women to come to the mixer.

7 ストレス解消にカラオケで歌う
I sing karaoke to release some stress.

8 ジムに通う
I go to the gym [regularly].

9 運動不足解消にランニングをする
I <u>run</u>/<u>jog</u> to make up for not getting enough exercise.

10 DVDを借りて帰る
I rent a DVD on my way home.

❺ mixer は主にアメリカで「男女混合の親睦会」の意味。
❼「カラオケ」は karaoke で通じるが、語尾の発音は [-ki] なので注意。
❾「運動不足だ」と言うなら I'm out of shape。
❿ I drop in the rental shop and <u>get</u>/<u>rent</u> a DVD on the way home. でも同じ意味。

chapter ⓾ After-Work Hours

11 異業種交流会に参加する
I take part in a cross-industrial exchange meeting.

12 同期と勉強会を開く
I hold a study session with my peers.

13 コンプライアンスについての社外セミナーに出席する
I attend a seminar on compliance outside the company.

14 パソコン教室に通い、基本的なPCスキルを身に付ける
I study at a computer training school and learn basic computer skills.

15 資格試験の勉強をする
I study to <u>pass</u>/<u>prepare for</u> a certification exam.

tips

⓫ take part in (参加する) はattend とも言い換えられる。
⓮「パソコン教室に通う」はI go to computer classes でもよい。
⓯ certification は「証明、検定」。「資格試験」はcertified qualification exam と言ってもよい。
⓰ keep oneself busy は「いつも忙しくしている」、work a second job で

16 副業に精を出す
I keep myself busy working a second job.

17 独立の準備をする
I prepare to set up a business of my own.

18 ボランティア活動に力を入れる
I'm actively involved in volunteer work.

19 駅でデートの待ち合わせをする
I promise to meet my boyfriend/girlfriend at the station for a date.

20 家でくつろぐ
I wind down at home.

「副業をする」。「本業」はone's day job/main occupation。
⓱ set up a business は「事業を始める」
⓲ be involved in ~ は「~に関わる、従事する」。「ボランティア活動」はvolunteer activities と言ってもよい。
⓴ wind down（[緊張が]緩む）はrelaxでも。wind[wáind]の発音に注意。

chapter 10 After-Work Hours

1. まだみんな残ってるから、帰りづらいなあ。
I can't leave with everyone still in the office.

2. 帰りがけに課長から残業頼まれちゃったよ〜。
The section chief asked me to work overtime just when I was about to leave.

3. 時には(たまには)一駅歩こうかな。
Maybe I should walk to the next station <u>sometimes</u> (<u>for a change</u>).

4. 毎日残業で、アフター5どころじゃないよ！
I work overtime every day and don't get to have a night life.

5. いやなことがあったから、今日はグチ聞いて！
I had such a bad day. Do you mind if I complain to you about it?

6. この一杯が明日の活力。
This will revitalize me to work tomorrow!

leave = 帰る、去る（過去・過去分詞形は**left**）／**with ~** = ～した状態で／**still** = まだ

「6時に（定時に）退社する」はI leave <u>work</u> /<u>the office</u> at <u>6:00 [o' clock]</u>(<u>on time</u>).。「早めに帰った」はI left work early.。

---

section chief = 課長／**ask ~ to ...** = ～に…するように頼む／**work overtime** = 残業する cf. overtime = 時間外[に]／**be about to ~** = まさに～しようとしている

「残業をする予定じゃなかった」はI wasn't planning on working overtime.、「昨日は2時間残業した」はI worked two hours overtime yesterday.。

---

walk to ~ = ～まで歩く／**next station** = 次の駅 cf. next stopとしてもよい／**for a change** = いつもと違って、珍しく

「健康のために毎日駅まで歩く」はI walk to the station every day to keep in shape.（keep in shape= 健康／体調を保つ）。

---

get to ~ = ～できる機会を得る／**night life** = ナイトライフ、夜遊び

後半はdon't have the chance to go out at night（夜遊びに行く機会がない）としてもよい。この場合はアフター5をそのままafter fiveとすると意味が通じなくなる。

---

such ~ = とても～／**have a bad day** = ついてない日だ、いやな一日だ／**Do you mind if ~ ?** = ～してもいいですか?／**complain** = 愚痴をこぼす、不満を言う

後半はCan I complain to you about it a little?、またはDo you mind if I complain about it for a little while? と言ってもよい。

---

revitalize = ～に新しい活力を与える cf. vitalize = ～を元気づける | vital = 活気のある、元気な

「一杯」はthisの代わりにa drinkと（または具体的にa beer<ビール一杯>のように）言ってもよい。「仕事のあとの一杯はうまい!」はA <u>drink</u>(<u>beer</u>) after work tastes so good!.。

chapter ⑩ After-Work Hours

7 最近の新人って付き合い悪いなあ。
Nowadays, new employees don't seem to want to go out with others.

8 大野さんは仕事中のイメージと違って、おしゃべりで気さくだなあ。
Unlike the image we have of her at work, Ms. Ohno is very talkative and easy to get along with.

9 彼、飲むと本音が出るのね。
When he drinks, he says what he's really thinking.

10 飲んでても仕事のことが頭から離れないよ。
I can't get work off my mind even though I'm having a drink.

11 よ〜し、今日は朝まで飲み明かすぞ!
OK! Let's drink till dawn!

12 すみません、下戸なんです。
Sorry, but I can't drink at all.

nowadays = 最近では、近頃／**new employee** = 新入社員／**seem to ~** = ~のように見える／**go out with~** = ~と付き合う cf. get along with ~ = ~と仲良くする | associate with ~ = ~と親しく交際する

「付き合いで飲みになんか行きたくない」は I don't want to go drinking just to socialize. と言う。

---

unlike ~ = ~とは違って／**image** = イメージ、印象／**at work** = 仕事中の cf. when she's workingでも同じ／**talkative** = 話し好きな、おしゃべりな／**easy to ~** = ~しやすい

「一度会ったら、彼女に対するイメージが変わった」は I changed my image of her after I met her once.。

---

what he's really thinking = 彼が本当に思っていること（whatは先行詞を含む関係代名詞<~すること>）

「本音と建前を使い分ける」は I separate my real feelings and what I do in public.。「彼の本音が知りたい」なら I want to know what he is really thinking.。

---

get ~ off one's mind = ~を忘れる／**even though ~** = ~にもかかわらず／**have a drink** = 一杯やる、酒を飲む

前半部分は I keep thinking about work「仕事のことを考え続けてしまう」と言うこともできる。

---

drink = 飲む、酒を飲む／**till dawn** = 明け方まで cf. dawn = 夜明け

「一晩中飲み明かそうよ」は Let's stay out drinking all night.。 飲みに誘うときは、「ちょっと一杯やりに行きましょう」なら Let's go for a drink.、「徹底的に飲もう」と誘う場合は Let's go drinking.。

Sorry, but ~ = 申し訳ないけれど~なんです cf. sorry = すみません／**not ~ at all** = 全く~ない

直訳すると「すみません、お酒は全く飲めないんです」。「お酒はあまり（そんなに）飲めない」なら I can't drink (that) much.。

chapter 10 After-Work Hours

13　割り勘にすると飲まない人が気の毒だよ。
If we split the bill, then it won't be fair to those who don't drink [alcohol].

14　部長が酔うと説教が始まるから、早く帰ろう。
Let's leave before the manager gets drunk and starts to lecture everyone.

15　もうこんな時間！　行かなきゃ。何とか抜けられないかな。
Look at the time! I really have to go. I wonder if I can get out somehow.

16　あ～あ、もう電車なくなっちゃったよ。
Shoot! I've missed the last train home.

17　今夜顔貸してくれない？　合コンの頭数がそろわないの。
Can you show up for the mixer tonight? We need to have the same number of men and women.

18　今夜の合コン、話の合う子いるかなあ。
I hope I can meet someone I can enjoy talking to at the mixer tonight.

split the bill = 割り勘にする cf. split = 割る、分配する／**be fair to ~** = ～に対して公平である cf. fair = 公平な／**those who don't drink [alcohol]** = お酒を飲まない人たち

直訳すると「割り勘にすると飲まない人たちに対して不公平だ／よくない」。

---

leave = 帰る cf. go homeでも同じ／**get drunk** = 酔っ払う／**lecture** = 説教する

「彼は酔っ払うと誰に対しても説教する癖がある」は He tends to lecture everyone when he gets drunk. となる。

Look at the time! = もうこんな時間だ! cf. the time = 時間、時刻／**have to go** = 行かなくてはならない cf. goの代わりにrunでもよい／**I wonder if ~** = ～かどうかと思う／**get out** = 外へ出る、出て行く／**somehow** = どうにかして、何とか

「もうこんな時間！」は I didn't know it was this late.（こんなに遅くなっているなんて気がつかなかった）でもよい。

Shoot! = しまった!、もう!／**miss** = 逃す／**the last train home** = 帰宅するための最終列車 cf. the last train = 終電

直訳すると「終電に乗り損ねてしまった」。「[帰りの]終電に乗れた、間に合った」なら I could catch the last train [home].。

---

show up for ~ = ～に出席する、顔を出す／**mixer** = 合コン cf.単に partyでも可／**need to ~** = ～する必要がある／**the same number of ~** = 同じ数の～

「男女同数そろってない」は We don't have the same number of men and women.。

---

meet = 出会う／**enjoy talking to ~** = ～と会話を楽しむ、楽しく話す

「あなたと話せてとても楽しかったです」と言うなら I really enjoyed talking with you.。「私たちには共通点がある（ない）」は We have something(nothing) in common.。

chapter ⑩ After-Work Hours

19 あ、今日のメンツはレベルが高いなあ。
Everyone at today's party is classy and good-looking.

20 ちょっと、女子が引いてるよ。
Hey, the girls aren't impressed.

21 本屋さんに寄って、新刊をチェックしてから帰ろう。
I'll stop by the bookstore and check the new titles/books.

22 ネイルサロン予約してるから、定時で上がるよ。
I'll leave the office on time because I have a reservation at the nail salon.

23 今日は、ライブに行くんで仕事を早く切り上げたの。
I cut my work short today to go to the concert.

24 待ち合わせに少し遅れそうだから、メールしておこう。
I'll send an e-mail saying I might be a little late for the meeting.

classy = しゃれた、格好いい／**good-looking** = ルックスがいい、きれいな cf. good-lookingは男女どちらにも使える | good-looking girl = 美人、good-looking guy = 二枚目、イケメン

直訳すると「今日のパーティは全員しゃれていて格好いい」となる。

Hey, = ねえ、ちょっと／**impressed** = 感心して、さすがだと思う cf. impress = 印象を与える、感動させる | I'm impressed. = すごいもんだ、感心しました

直訳は「女子は感心していない」。「あきれ返っている」なら The girls are disgusted.。

---

stop by = 立ち寄る／**bookstore** = 書店／**the new title** = 新刊 cf. title = 題名、書名、本

「私はよく立ち読みする」なら I often browse books in the bookstore.。

---

leave the office on time = 定時に退社する／**have a reservation** = 予約がある／**nail salon** = ネイルサロン cf. nailist = ネイリスト

後半は I have a reservation to get my nails done.（ネイルの予約をしている）でもよい。get one's nails done は「爪の手入れをしてもらう、マニキュアを塗ってもらう」。

---

cut ~ short = ~を途中で切り上げる、短くする／**concert** = コンサート cf. 通常、生の実演で行われるので、これだけでライブと同じ意味。英語のliveは「生で、実演で」。

「今日、早退してもいいですか？」と言うには Can I leave early today?、「早退しなくてはならない」は I have to leave [the office] early.。

---

send an e-mail = メールを送る／**I might be ~** = ~するかもしれない／**a little late for ~** = ~に少し遅れる／**meeting** = 集まり、会合

「彼女と7時に駅前で待ち合わせする」は I'll meet my girlfriend in front of the station at 7:00.。

chapter ⑩ After-Work Hours

25 あの人、さっきから全然マイクを離さないんだけど。
That <u>guy/woman</u> just keeps singing and never gives up the microphone.

26 忘れてた！ 今日はヨガ教室の日だ！
Oh, I forgot! I have my yoga class today!

27 デスクワークでなまった体を動かすのは気持ちいい。
I feel great when I work out, because I work mostly at my desk and hardly ever move around.

28 アフター5は自分磨きにあてなきゃね。
I should spend after-work hours improving myself.

29 キャリアアップしようと思ったら何か資格を取らないと。
I need to have qualifications of some sort if I want to advance my career.

30 年を取ると、新しいことへのチャレンジがおっくうになるな……。
As I get older, I don't often feel like trying anything new.

keep ~ing = 〜し続ける／give up ~ = 〜を手放す、放棄する／microphone = マイク

後半は「ほかの誰にもマイクを渡そうとしない」never passes the microphone to anyone else と言い換えてもよい。

I forgot! = 忘れていた！（forgotはforgetの過去形）／have class = クラスがある cf. have my yoga lessonとしても同じ

「ヨガ教室があるのを忘れてた！」なら I forgot I had my yoga class [today]!。「〜を思い出した」は I remember〜。

---

feel great = 気持ちがいい、いい気分である／work out = 運動する／work at one's desk = デスクに向かって仕事をする、事務をする／mostly = たいていは、ほとんど／hardly ever ~ = ほとんど〜ない、めったに〜ない／move around = 動き回る

直訳すると「運動すると気持ちいい、ほとんどデスクでの仕事で動かないから」。「ほとんど動かない」は I hardly move at all と言っても同じ。

---

spend = 過ごす、費やす／after-work hours = 仕事の後の時間、アフター5／improve oneself = 自分自身を向上させる

「自分の能力を磨き直す」は brush up one's skills、「〜についての知識に磨きをかける」は improve one's knowledge of ~ と言う。

---

qualification = 資格／of some sort = 何らかの cf. sort = 種類／**advance one's career = キャリアを積む、出世する** cf. advance = 〜を前へ進める、前進させる

「キャリアアップしたければ」は if I want a better career（よりよいキャリアを望むなら）でもよい。

---

as ~ = 〜するにつれて／get older = 年を取る cf. get old = 年寄りになる／**don't feel like ~ = 〜したい気持ちにならない／try anything new = 何か新しいことに挑戦する**

「何か新しいことをやってみれば？」は Why don't you try something new?。

chapter 10 After-Work Hours

31 今のままではリストラされちゃう。手に職をつけないと。
If things go on as they are now, I might lose my job. I need to have some marketable skills.

32 社外の人と会うのは、刺激になる。
It's really <u>inspiring</u>/<u>stimulating</u> to meet [and talk with] people from other companies.

33 名刺を補充しておかなきゃ。
I have to restock my business cards.

34 今日はどんな業界の人が来てるんだろう。
Those people who came here today... I wonder what industry they're from.

35 帰ったらすぐゲームの続きやらなきゃ。これって依存症?
I have to continue my video game as soon as I get home. Am I addicted to video games?

36 今日は冷凍食品半額デーだから、スーパーに寄って帰ろう。
I will stop by the supermarket because frozen food is half-price today.

if things go on as they are = この調子では、このまま行くと cf. go on = 進み続ける／**I might ~** = 私は~するかもしれない／**lose one's job** = 職を失う／**have marketable skills** = 手に職がある cf. marketable = 売り物になる

「リストラ」は restructuring の略だが、ここでの「リストラされる」は「失業する」という意味で訳している。

It's really ~ to ... = … するのは本当に~だ／**inspiring** = 活気づける、影響を与えてくれる／**stimulating** = 刺激的な、よい刺激になる／**people from other companies** = ほかの会社の人たち

「初対面の人に会う」は meet someone new。

---

restock = 補充する cf. stock = 蓄える、入れる／**business card** = 名刺

「名刺入れに名刺を入れる」は I put business cards into a [card] holder/case.。「名刺を切らしてしまった」は I ran out of my business cards.。

I wonder ~ = ~かと思う／**industry** = 業界 cf. companies from different industries = 異なった業種の会社

直訳すると「今日来ている人たち、どんな業界から来ているんだろう」。

---

continue = 続ける／**video game** = ビデオゲーム(テレビゲーム、パソコンゲーム <PC game>などが含まれる)／**as soon as ~** = ~するとすぐに／**be addicted to ~** = ~の中毒になっている、~に夢中になっている cf. addict = 熱中させる、依存症

後半部分は Am I a video game addict? でもよい。video game addict は「テレビゲーム中毒、病みつきになっている人」。

---

stop by ~ = ~に立ち寄る／**supermarket** = スーパーマーケット(英語では superと省略しない)／**frozen food** = 冷凍食品／**half-price** = 半額

「特売日」は bargain/sale day、「お買い得だ」は It's a bargain. と言う。

chapter 10 After-Work Hours

37 夕食はまたコンビニ弁当か。
Another dinner from the convenience store!

38 あ、録画予約し忘れた！
Oh, no! I forgot to have that TV program recorded!

39 気になってたあのドラマを一気に借りるぞ〜！
I'm going to rent that whole drama series I've been so curious to watch!

40 今夜こそあのDVD観ないと延滞になっちゃう！
I have to watch that DVD tonight [and return it] or I'll have to pay a late fee.

41 仕事と遊びの両立が永遠のテーマだな。
Trying to balance out work and play is always my biggest challenge.

another ~ = またいつもと同じ〜、例によって／dinner = 夕食、食事／convenience store = コンビニエンスストア、コンビニ（英語では省略できない）

はっきり「弁当」と言いたければ boxed meal [from the convenience store]。「コンビニ弁当ばかりでは体によくないのはわかってる」なら I know it's not good for me to live on those convenience store dinners.。

I forgot to ~ = 〜するのを忘れた（forgotはforgetの過去形）／have ~ recorded = 〜を録画しておく cf. record = 録画する

反対に「その番組は録画してある」なら、I have that program recorded.。

---

rent = [お金を出して]借りる／whole = 全部、丸ごと／drama series = 連続ドラマ cf. series = 連続、シリーズ／**be curious to ~ = 〜してみたくてたまらない** cf. curious = 好奇心をそそる、気になる

「新作DVDを借りてきた」は I rented a new DVD.。「観たいDVDは全部貸し出し中だった」なら All the DVDs I wanted to see were rented out.。

---

watch DVD = DVDを観る／return = 返却する／or ~ = さもないと〜／pay = 支払う／late fee = 延滞料 cf. fee = 料金

「DVDを2日遅れで店に返却する」なら return the DVD to the rental store two days overdue。overdue は「期限を過ぎた」。

---

balance out = バランスを保つ／challenge = 挑戦、課題

ここでは「テーマ」を「やり遂げたいと思っていること」として、英語では「仕事と遊びのバランスを取ることが常に最大の課題」と訳している。

Skit アフター5編

アクティブ派 VS ひきこもり派

Woman: **Hey, how was your weekend?**
Man: **I rented a DVD on my way home and watched it on Saturday.**
W: **You have no social life❶.**
M: **What do you mean?❷**
W: **On Saturday, I went to the gym and then went bar hopping with friends.**
M: **I stopped by the bookstore and checked the new titles on Sunday.**
W: **How thrilling❸. I studied at a computer training school and did some volunteer activities.**
M: **Well, I like to relax at home.**
W: **Can I ask you out for a drink tonight? We could sing karaoke to release some stress.**
M: **Sorry, I can't drink at all.**
W: **Oh, I forgot. I have my yoga lesson tonight.**
M: **You have the gym, bars, computer school, volunteering, karaoke and yoga. I have DVDs and books. You're right. I have no social life.**

女性：ねえ、週末はどうだった？
男性：帰りにDVDを借りて、土曜日に観たよ。
女：社会と隔絶してるわね。
男：どういうこと？
女：土曜日に、私はジムに行って、友達とバーをはしごしてたわ。
男：日曜日は本屋さんに寄って、新刊をチェックしてたよ。
女：まあ、スリル満点だこと。私はコンピューター教室へ行って、それからボランティア活動をしてたわ。
男：いやあ、僕は家でくつろぐのが好きでね。
女：今夜、飲みに行かない？ ストレス解消にカラオケで歌ったりして。
男：悪いけど、僕は下戸なんだ。
女：あ、忘れてた。今夜はヨガのレッスンだったんだわ。
男：君は、ジムやバーにコンピューター教室、ボランティアやカラオケやヨガにも行ってるわけだ。僕はDVDと本。認めるよ、確かに僕は社会と隔絶してるよ。

【語 注】

❶ social life: 社会生活、社交生活
❷ What do you mean?: （相手の言ったことを受けて）それはどういう意味ですか
❸ thrilling: スリルがある、ゾクゾクする

Quick Check

本章に出てきたフレーズを復習しましょう。以下の日本語の意味になるよう英文を完成させてください。答えはページの下にあります。

❶ 飲んで憂さを晴らす。 ➡P262
I ( ) ( ) my troubles.

❷ 運動不足解消にランニングをする。 ➡P263
I run/jog to ( ) ( ) ( ) not getting enough exercise.

❸ 副業に精を出す。 ➡P265
I ( ) myself ( ) working a ( ) job.

❹ まだみんな残ってるから、帰りづらいなあ。 ➡P266
I can't ( ) ( ) everyone ( ) in the office.

❺ 飲んでても仕事のことが頭から離れないよ。 ➡P268
I can't ( ) work ( ) ( ) ( ) even though I'm having a drink.

❻ あ〜あ、もう電車なくなっちゃったよ。 ➡P270
Shoot! I've ( ) ( ) ( ) ( ) home.

❼ 今日は、ライブに行くんで仕事を早く切り上げたの。 ➡P272
I ( ) my work ( ) today to go to the concert.

❽ キャリアアップしようと思ったら何か資格を取らないと。 ➡P274
I need to have ( ) of some sort if I want to ( ) ( ) ( ).

❾ 年を取ると、新しいことへのチャレンジがおっくうになるな……。 ➡P274
As I ( ) ( ), I don't often ( ) ( ) ( ) anything new.

❿ 帰ったらすぐゲームの続きやらなきゃ。これって依存症? ➡P276
I have to ( ) my video game ( ) ( ) ( ) I get home. Am I ( ) ( ) video games?

---

❶drink/away ❷make/up/for ❸keep/busy/second ❹leave/with/still ❺get/off/my/mind ❻missed/the/last/train ❼cut/short ❽qualifications/advance/my/career ❾get/older/feel/like/trying ❿continue/as/soon/as/addicted/to

［完全改訂版］
起きてから寝るまで英語表現700 オフィス編

2010年3月11日 初版発行

監修　吉田研作
執筆・解説　武藤克彦／荒井貴和

監修　吉田研作
上智大学外国語学部英語学科教授。専門は応用言語学。文部科学省中央教育審議会外国語専門部会委員。J-SHINE理事・認定委員長。「起きてから寝るまで」シリーズ発刊当初より監修を務める。著書に『どうなる小学校英語──「必修化」のゆくえ』（共著、アルク）など多数。

執筆・解説（体の動き・行為／つぶやき表現）

武藤克彦（むとうかつひこ）Chap 1,3,5,7,9
上智大学大学院修了（言語学）。大学・高校・企業等での英語教育指導を経て、現在は獨協大学外国語教育研究所講師。著書に『起きてから寝るまで英単語帳』『起きてから寝るまで英語表現700』（両書とも共著、アルク）『はじめての起きてから寝るまで英語表現　男性編』（アルク）『スピード攻略できるTOEICテストパーフェクト模試』（共著、桐原書店）など。

荒井貴和（あらいきわ）Chap 2,4,6,8,10
上智大学非常勤講師、元東洋学園大学助教授。専門は英語教育・応用言語学。著書に『TOEFLグラマー』（荒竹出版）『新装版　起きてから寝るまで英会話まるごと練習帳』『起きてから寝るまで英単語帳』『起きてから寝るまで英語表現700』（両書とも共著、アルク）『起きてから寝るまで英語表現　女性編』（アルク）『あたらしい英語科教育法』（共著、学文社）など。

英文校正：Owen Schaefer、Joel Weinberg、Peter Branscombe
Skit作成：Eda Sterner

AD・デザイン：遠藤 紅（アレフ・ゼロ）
表紙イラスト：おおの麻里
本文イラスト：飯山和哉・石坂しづか（単語編）

CDナレーション：Julia Yermakov、Carolyn Miller、Howard Colefield、Soness Stevens、Jeffrey Rowe、島ゆうこ
録音・編集：中録サービス株式会社／ログスタジオ／安西一明
CD制作：ソニー・ミュージック コミュニケーションズ

DTP：朝日メディアインターナショナル株式会社
印刷・製本：広研印刷株式会社

発行人：平本照麿
発行所：株式会社アルク
〒168-8611　東京都杉並区永福2-54-12
TEL：03-3327-1101（カスタマーサービス部）
TEL：03-3323-2444（英語出版編集部）
アルクの出版情報：
http://www.alc.co.jp/publication/
編集部e-mailアドレス：shuppan@alc.co.jp

乱丁本、落丁本が発生した場合は、弊社にてお取り替えいたしております。弊社カスタマーサービス部（電話：03-3327-1101 受付時間：平日9時〜17時）までご相談ください。　定価はカバーに表示しております。

©Kensaku Yoshida, Katsuhiko Muto, Kiwa Arai, ALC Press, Inc. 2010
Printed in Japan　PC: 7009171

アルクのキャラクターです　WOWI（ウォーウィ）
WOWIは、WORLDWIDEから生まれたアルクのシンボルキャラクターです。温かなふれあいを求める人間の心を象徴する、見わたし、地球人のシンボルです。
http://alcom.alc.co.jp/
学んで教える人材育成コミュニティ・サイト

詳しい資料を無料で差し上げます！

目的・レベル別に選べる！
アルクの通信講座は充実のラインアップ

レベル		入門／初級			中級		上級	
英 検	5級	4級	3級	準2級	2級	準1級	1級	
TOEIC	–	–	350点	470点	600点	730点	860点	
TOEFL	(iBT)		32点	46点	61点	80点	100点	

聞く力をつけたい
- ヒアリングマラソン・ベーシック kikuzo!　英語聞き取りのコツをつかむ！
- 日常会話へステップアップ。　ヒアリングマラソン中級コース
- 100万人が実感した、人気ナンバーワン講座。**1000時間ヒアリングマラソン**

聞く・話す力をつけたい
- 英語の耳と口を徹底して鍛える。　リピーティングマラソン
- もっと英語らしく、もっと自由に話したい！　リピーティングマラソン実践コース
- 21種類の通訳トレーニング法で英語力を強化！　通訳トレーニング入門
- あなたの発音を「ナオスケ」が診断。　ヒアリング力完成 発音トレーニング

話す力をつけたい
- イングリッシュ キング　1日20分×週3日の新英会話習慣！
- 英会話コエダス　ブリティッシュ　イギリス英語を身につけたい！
- 英会話コエダス　持ち歩ける英会話スクール。
- イメージどおりに英語を操る！　英会話コエダス・アドバンス

ビジネス英語を学びたい
- もう一度英語　ビジネス Basic　1日15分！ 英語の基礎を総復習。
- 学校英語をビジネス仕様に磨き上げ！　もう一度英語　ビジネス Chance
- クリエイティブに会話を操る！　ビジネス英会話 クリダス
- プレゼン・会議・交渉の英語に自信をつけたい！　ヒアリングマラソン ビジネス

TOEICテストに備えたい
- TOEIC®テスト 超入門キット　1日15分、聞くだけで身につく！
- TOEIC®テスト 470点入門マラソン　1日30分×週4日の学習で英語力の下地を作る。
- 奪取550点 TOEIC®テスト 解答テクニック講座　スコア直結の解答テクニックを手に入れる！
- 海外出張をこなせる力を養成。　TOEIC®テスト 650点突破マラソン
- TOEICのプロが奥義を伝授！　奪取730点 TOEIC®テスト 攻略プログラム
- ビジネスで勝負できる本物の英語力を。　TOEIC®テスト 800点攻略プログラム
- 目標はノンネイティブ最高レベル！　挑戦900点 TOEIC®テスト攻略プログラム

※各講座のレベルは目安です。

資料(無料)のご請求は下記フリーダイヤルまたはインターネットで

お電話　アルク・フリーダイヤル
0120-120-800
※携帯電話・PHSからもご利用いただけます。　(24時間受付)

インターネット　アルク・オンラインショップ
http://shop.alc.co.jp/
アルクの通信講座全ラインアップや講座の詳細もご覧頂けます。

※お知らせいただいた個人情報は、資料の発送および小社からの商品情報をお送りするために利用し、その目的以外での使用はいたしません。
また、お客様の個人情報に変更の必要がある場合は、カスタマーサービス部(TEL. 03-3327-1101)までご連絡をお願い申しあげます。

〒168-8611 東京都杉並区永福2-54-12　**株式会社 アルク**

アルク
www.alc.co.jp

128のKey表現で、日常会話に自信が持てる!
英会話 コエダス

道案内や電話応対など、実用的な表現を繰り返しコエダス(声に出す)してマスターします。アルクが誇る2つのデータベースから、「日本人が英語を必要とする場面」と、「必要になるフレーズ」を厳選。日常生活を網羅する表現を身につければ、自信を持って英語を話せます!

受講開始レベル	TOEIC350点程度/英検3級
受講料	29,589円(税込)

2つのデータベースから
実用的な「128のKey表現」を厳選

学習者約1,000人にアンケートを実施し、英語が必要な「32の場面」を選定。その場面でよく使われる表現を、スポークンコーパス※1で分析しました。さらに、学習者コーパス※2を使って間違いやすいポイントを分析。こうして選定されたのが、実用性の高い「128のKey表現」です。当講座ではこの128の表現を、声に出して確実にマスターします。

※1 ネイティブ・スピーカーの話し言葉のデータベース
※2 日本人が話す英語のデーターベース

置き換え表現 64
「○○するつもり」など、一部を置き換えて表現の幅を広げるフレーズ

丸覚え表現 64
「お邪魔します」「少々待ちください」など、覚えればそのまま使えるフレーズ

厳選した使用頻度の高い 128のKey表現

「置き換え表現」をマスターすれば、あなたの英会話がスピーディーに!

ネイティブ・スピーカーと自然な速さで会話するには、日本語で考えてから英訳していたのでは間に合いません。当講座では、64の「置き換え表現」を使って、CDに収録された問いかけにテンポよく答えたり、表現を即座に言い換えたりする練習に取り組みます。こうすることで英語の反射神経が鍛えられ、スピード感あふれる英会話ができるようになります。

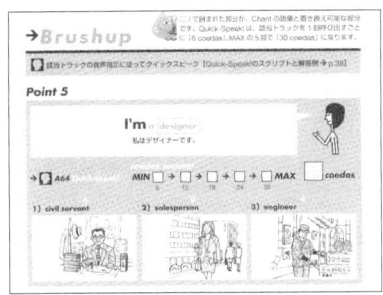

イラストや音声に即座に反応して、英語をすぐに声に出す!

多彩な練習法で、会話力を効果的にアップ!

当講座は、声に出す練習が中心ですが、ただ音読するだけではすぐに飽きてしまいます。そこで、リピーティングやロールプレイなど、さまざまな練習法を組み合わせて、体系的に学ぶカリキュラムを用意しました。学習テーマも身近なものばかり。楽しく続けられ、英語を口にする抵抗感がなくなります。机に向かわなくてもできる手軽さも、人気の一因です。

4カ月の学習テーマ（抜粋）

- ➔ 道案内できますか?
- ➔ えっ!なんて言ったの?
- ➔ どのツアーがお勧めですか?
- ➔ エアコンが壊れてる?
- ➔ やっぱりショッピング
- ➔ 空港でお出迎え
- ➔ ツアーガイドを体験!
- ➔ お見積りをお願いします

「英会話コエダス」で、あなたの英会話をもっと自由に!

教材構成
コースガイド1冊／テキスト4冊／CD8枚／別冊フレーズ集『Key128』（CD付き）1冊／マンスリーテスト4回／特製CDケース1個／修了証（修了時に発行）

講 座 名	英会話コエダス
商品コード	S5
標準学習期間	4カ月
学習時間の目安	1日40分×週4日
受 講 料	29,589円（税込）
お支払い方法	クレジットカード（一括・分割） 代金引換（一括のみ、手数料420円） コンビニ・郵便払込（一括のみ、手数料無料）

お申し込み受付後、3営業日以内に、教材を一括で配送センターより出荷いたします。

お申し込みは、以下の方法で!

■ 通話料無料のフリーダイヤル
0120-120-800
24時間受付。携帯電話・PHSからも承ります。

■ アルク・オンラインショップ
http://shop.alc.co.jp/

身近なことを表現できる英語力が身につく

ひとりでできる英会話
起きてから寝るまで シリーズ

アルク
www.alc.co.␣

日常のひとコマを「英語でつぶやく」ことで口から自然と英語が出てくるようになる「起きてから寝るまで」シリーズ。あなたもこの「つぶやき」学習法、始めてみませんか?

時代の声にこたえて進化!
完全改訂版
起きてから寝るまで
英語表現 700
本+CD1枚 1,680円 (税込)

海外旅行がもっと楽しくなる
新装版
起きてから寝るまで表現 550
海外旅行編
本+CD1枚 1,554円 (税込)

日常単語はこれでバッチリ
起きてから寝るまで
英単語帳
本+CD1枚 1,890円 (税込)

子育て中も英語でエクササイズ
新装版
起きてから寝るまで
子育て表現 550
本+CD1枚 1,554円 (税込)

英語で言いたい表現を2200以上も収録
起きてから寝るまで
英語表現ミニ辞典
本+CD2枚 1,974円 (税込)

「つぶやき」を続けて口慣らし!
新装版
起きてから寝るまで
英会話口慣らし練習帳
本+CD2枚 1,974円 (税込)

基本表現をくりかえし練習
新装版
起きてから寝るまで
英会話まるごと練習帳
本+CD2枚 1,974年 (税込)

お近くの書店にてお求めください。
書店にない場合は、小社に直接お申し込みください。

㈱アルク　〒168-8611 東京都杉並区永福2-54-12

0120-120-800　通話料無料のフリーダイヤル (24時間受付)
※ 携帯電話、PHSからも承ります

アルク・オンラインショップ http://shop.alc.co.jp/

日常生活を英語で表現
起きてから寝るまで表現 550
日常生活編
本+CD1枚 1,554円 (税込)

※ 小社に直接ご注文の場合、1回あたりの合計額が3,150円 (税込) 未満の場合は、発送手数料150円 (税込) を申し受けます。
※ 2010年1月現在の情報です。